INDIA 2016 HUMAN RIGHTS REPORT

EXECUTIVE SUMMARY

India is a multiparty, federal, parliamentary democracy with a bicameral parliament. The president, elected by an electoral college, is the head of state, and the prime minister is the head of the government. Under the constitution, the 29 states and seven union territories have a high degree of autonomy and have primary responsibility for law and order. Voters elected President Pranab Mukherjee in 2012 to a five-year term, and Narendra Modi became prime minister following the victory of the National Democratic Alliance coalition led by the Bharatiya Janata Party in the May 2014 general elections. Observers considered these elections, which included more than 551 million participants, free and fair, despite isolated instances of violence.

Civilian authorities maintained effective control over the security forces.

The most significant human rights problems involved instances of police and security force abuses, including extrajudicial killings, torture, and rape; corruption, which remained widespread and contributed to ineffective responses to crimes, including those against women, children, and members of Scheduled Castes (SCs) or Scheduled Tribes (STs); and societal violence based on gender, religious affiliation, and caste or tribe.

Other human rights problems included disappearances, hazardous prison conditions, arbitrary arrest and detention, and lengthy pretrial detention. Court backlogs delayed or denied justice, including through lengthy pretrial detention and denial of due process. The government placed restrictions on foreign funding of nongovernmental organizations (NGOs), including some whose views the government believed were not in the "national or public interest," curtailing the work of civil society. There were instances of infringement of privacy rights. The law in six states restricted religious conversion, and there were reports of arrests but no reports of convictions under those laws. Some limits on the freedom of movement continued. Rape, domestic violence, dowry-related deaths, honor killings, sexual harassment, and discrimination against women and girls remained serious societal problems. Child abuse, female genital mutilation and cutting, and forced and early marriage were problems. Trafficking in persons, including widespread bonded and forced labor of children and adults, and sex trafficking of children and adults for prostitution, were serious problems. Societal discrimination against persons with disabilities and indigenous persons continued, as did discrimination and violence based on gender identity, sexual orientation, and persons with HIV.

A lack of accountability for misconduct at all levels of government persisted, contributing to widespread impunity. Investigations and prosecutions of individual cases took place, but lax enforcement, a shortage of trained police officers, and an overburdened and under resourced court system contributed to infrequent convictions.

Separatist insurgents and terrorists in Jammu and Kashmir, the northeastern states, and the Maoist belt committed serious abuses, including killings of armed forces personnel, police, government officials, and civilians.

Section 1. Respect for the Integrity of the Person, Including Freedom from:

a. Arbitrary Deprivation of Life and other Unlawful or Politically Motivated Killings

There were reports the government and its agents committed arbitrary or unlawful killings, including extrajudicial killings of suspected criminals and insurgents. During the year the South Asian Terrorism Portal (SATP), run by the nonprofit Institute for Conflict Management, reported fatalities due to terrorism and insurgency (other than Maoist extremism), to include 145 civilians, 114 security force members, and 324 terrorists or insurgents. According to the SATP, fatalities due to terrorist violence in the northeastern states decreased from 273 deaths in 2015 to 119 during the year. Data compiled by the Institute of Conflict Management showed fatalities from terrorist violence in Jammu and Kashmir increased to 223 between January and October 2016 compared with 174 in 2015. Furthermore, the 2016 figure does not include 90 persons, including violent protesters, reportedly killed by security forces during a four-month period of unrest in the summer.

There were 104 reported police "encounter deaths"--a term used to describe any encounter between the security or police forces and alleged criminals or insurgents that results in a death--registered countrywide by the Investigation Division of the National Human Rights Commission (NHRC), according to Ministry of Home Affairs 2015 data. The Telangana government established a special investigation team to investigate the April 2015 deaths of five prisoners killed by police in Nalgonda District, Telangana, while being transported to a court in Hyderabad for trial. At the year's end, the special investigation team had yet to submit its report to the High Court of Judicature at Hyderabad.

In August 2015 the NHRC ordered the central government to pay 500,000 rupees ($7,500) as compensation for the 2011 Border Security Force killing of Felani Khatun. During the year the central government rejected the NHRC recommendation and did not pay the compensation. Felani's family and Kolkata-based rights group MASUM petitioned the Supreme Court against the government's refusal to pay compensation.

On August 8, Telangana security personnel fatally shot an individual, described by police as a former Maoist insurgent, who was a witness in an alleged 2005 "encounter" case involving a joint Rajasthan and Gujarat antiterrorism squad. A special Central Bureau of Investigation (CBI) court trial in Mumbai continued its deliberations on the 2005 case.

On October 31, Madhya Pradesh police reportedly killed eight suspected members of the outlawed Students' Islamic Movement of India, after they allegedly murdered a prison guard and escaped from the high-security Central Jail of Bhopal. On November 1, the NHRC issued a formal complaint against the state government, police, and prison authorities, expressing concern about deaths. The Madhya Pradesh police appointed a special investigation team to investigate the killings.

There continued to be reports of custodial death cases, in which prisoners or detainees were killed or died in police custody. Decisions by central and state authorities not to prosecute police or security officials despite reports of evidence in certain cases remained a problem. The National Crime Records Bureau (NCRB) reported 97 cases of custodial deaths in 2015 with Maharashtra reporting the highest number of cases at 19. Uttar Pradesh reported nine cases and Punjab three cases.

On March 14, the Tamil Nadu government awarded 500,000 rupees ($7,500) compensation to relatives of an auto-rickshaw driver after determining a Nagapattinam District police inspector used excessive force, which led to the driver's death in 2014. The Madras High Court oversaw the departmental inquiry after the NGO Campaign for Custodial Justice and Abolition of Torture filed a public interest petition in April 2014. Criminal and departmental proceedings against the inspector were pending.

On April 9, 20-year-old Sunil Yadav was found dead in Umri police station in Madhya Pradesh, four days after his arrest on charges of theft. Madhya Pradesh police suspended four police personnel and ordered a judicial inquiry.

The Armed Forces Special Powers Act (AFSPA) remained in effect in Nagaland, Manipur, Assam, and parts of Mizoram, and a version of the law was in effect in Jammu and Kashmir. Under the AFSPA, a central government designation of state or union territory as a "disturbed area," authorizes security forces in the state to use deadly force to "maintain law and order" and arrest any person "against whom reasonable suspicion exists" without informing the detainee of the grounds for arrest. The law also provides security forces immunity from civilian prosecution for acts committed in regions under the AFSPA. There were no official records available of enforcement actions or human rights abuses by security forces under the AFSPA during the year. In September the central government denied a request to visit Jammu and Kashmir by the Office of the UN High Commissioner for Human Rights and the NHRC. The government also denied NHRC access to Manipur.

There was considerable public support for repeal of the AFSPA, particularly in areas that experienced a significant decrease in insurgent attacks. On July 8, the Supreme Court ruled 1,528 alleged "encounter" cases in Manipur during the last 20 years must be investigated and armed forces personnel should not be immune from prosecution if the investigations disclosed criminal conduct. The ruling stated the indefinite deployment of armed forces under AFSPA "mocks India's democratic process."

On August 9, human rights activist Irom Sharmila ended her 16-year hunger strike to protest of the imposition of AFSPA in Manipur. Sharmila remained in police custody for 16 years for violating a law that criminalizes attempted suicide. She initiated her strike after federal paramilitary forces killed 10 civilians in 2000.

On June 17, a Gujarat special court convicted 24 individuals (11 of whom were sentenced to life imprisonment), and acquitted 36 others for their role in the Gulberg Society killings in 2002, when a rioting mob killed 69 individuals during communal unrest. A separate case filed by Zakia Jafri one of the Gulberg Society survivors, remained pending in the Gujarat High Court. The High Court also affirmed a 2013 lower court verdict exonerating senior Gujarat government officials from culpability in the communal violence that engulfed the state from February to May 2002.

Nongovernmental forces, including organized insurgents and terrorists, committed numerous killings and bombings in Punjab, Jammu and Kashmir, the northeastern states, and the Maoist belt (see section 1.g.). Maoists in Jharkhand and Bihar continued to attack security forces and key infrastructure facilities such as railways and communication towers. On July 19, Maoist rebels conducted improvised explosive device attacks, killing 10 paramilitary soldiers on the border of Gaya and Aurangabad districts in Bihar.

b. Disappearance

There were allegations police failed to file required arrest reports for detained persons, resulting in hundreds of unresolved disappearances. Police and government officials denied these claims. The central government reported that state government screening committees informed families about the status of detainees. There were reports, however, that prison guards sometimes required bribes from families to confirm the detention of their relatives.

Disappearances attributed to government forces, paramilitary forces, and insurgents occurred in areas of conflict during the year (see section 1.g.).

c. Torture and Other Cruel, Inhuman, or Degrading Treatment or Punishment

The law prohibits torture, but NGOs reported torture occurred during the year.

Police beatings of prisoners resulted in custodial deaths (see section 1.a.).

The law does not permit authorities to admit coerced confessions into evidence, but NGOs and citizens alleged authorities used torture to coerce confessions. In some instances authorities submitted these confessions as evidence in capital cases. Authorities allegedly also used torture as a means to extort money or as summary punishment. According to human rights experts, the government continued to try individuals arrested and charged under the repealed Prevention of Terrorism Act and Terrorist and Disruptive Activities Act. Under the repealed law, authorities treated a confession made to a police officer as admissible as evidence in court.

According to a National Law University, Delhi study released in May, a significant percentage of prisoners on death row reported that they lived in inhumane conditions, were denied due process, and were subjected to torture. The university's Death Penalty Research Project interviewed 373 of 385 current death row inmates between July 2013 and January 2015. Of the 270 prisoners who spoke about their experience in police custody, 216 said they had been tortured. Among states with 10 or more death row prisoners, Haryana had the highest proportion of those that reported being tortured in custody. The study categorized three out of four death row inmates as "economically vulnerable" and indicated social and economic factors often determined how authorities treated a person in jail.

On July 8, police arrested environmental and human rights activist Piyush Manush and his associates, Esan Karthik and Muthu, for protesting the construction of a railway overpass in Salem, Tamil Nadu. The court granted bail to Karthik and Muthu on July 15. Manush did not receive bail and NGOs alleged that while in Salem Central Prison police bound his hands, beat him, and placed him in solitary confinement. On July 24, the NHRC issued a notice to the Tamil Nadu government requesting a response to the allegations.

On April 5, the Supreme Court granted bail to disabled Delhi University professor G.N. Saibaba on medical grounds after Maharashtra police arrested him in 2014 for alleged links with Maoist insurgents and for violating the Unlawful Activities Prevention Act (UAPA). In 2014 Amnesty International and civil rights activists campaigned for Saibaba's release and alleged jail authorities denied him medical and sanitary facilities.

In January the CBI charged two police officials in Dharavi, Maharashtra with culpable homicide after a detainee died, allegedly from multiple injuries inflicted by the officers. Police initially claimed his death was due to meningitis. In June 2014 the Bombay High Court instructed CBI to takeover the investigation from the Mumbai Crime Branch.

There were continued reports that police raped male and female detainees. The government authorized the NHRC to investigate rape cases involving police officers. By law the NHRC can also request information about cases involving the army and paramilitary forces, but it has no mandate to investigate those cases. NGOs claimed the NHRC underestimated the number of rapes committed in police custody. Some rape victims were unwilling to report crimes due to social stigma and the possibility of retribution, compounded by a perception of a lack of oversight and accountability, especially if the perpetrator was a police officer or other official. There were reports police officials refused to register rape cases.

In April Kanyakumari District police arrested and detained 17 persons from the Kurava tribal community for alleged theft. According to local NGOs, police allegedly beat, tortured, and sexually assaulted the detainees over a period of 63 days. On July 8, the Tamil Nadu State Human Rights Commission initiated a probe into the conduct of the Kanyakumari Police.

Prison and Detention Center Conditions

Prison conditions were frequently life threatening and did not meet international standards.

Physical Conditions: Prisons were often severely overcrowded, and food, medical care, sanitation, and environmental conditions often were inadequate. Potable water was only occasionally available. Prisons and detention centers remained underfunded, understaffed, and lacking sufficient infrastructure. Prisoners were physically mistreated.

According to the NCRB *Prison Statistics India 2015* report, there were 1,401 prisons in the country with an authorized capacity of 366,781 persons. The actual incarcerated population was 419,623. Persons awaiting trial accounted for more than two-thirds of the prison population. Authorities held men and women separately. The law requires the detention of juveniles in rehabilitative facilities, although at times authorities detained them in adult prisons, especially in rural areas. Authorities often detained pretrial detainees along with convicted prisoners. In Uttar Pradesh, occupancy at most prisons was two and sometimes three times the permitted capacity, according to an advisor appointed by the Supreme Court.

According to NCRB, authorities convicted three out of an estimated 600 inmates in a prison in Dantewada, Chhattisgarh. The remainder of prisoners awaited trial in a jail built for a capacity of 150. According to the NCRB 2015 report, overcrowding was most severe in Dadra and Nagar Haveli at 277 percent of capacity, while Chhattisgarh prisons were at 234 percent of capacity; and Delhi prisons at 227 percent of capacity. A 2016 study on Indian prison monitoring by Commonwealth Human Rights Initiative cited little oversight of prisons, neglect of facilities, and breaches of prisoner rights.

Administration: Authorities permitted visitors some access to prisoners, although some family members claimed authorities denied access to relatives, particularly in conflict areas, including Jammu and Kashmir. There was no ombudsman for detention facilities, but authorities allowed prisoners to submit complaints to judicial authorities.

Independent Monitoring: The NHRC received and investigated prisoner complaints of human rights violations throughout the year, but civil society representatives believed few prisoners filed complaints due to fear of retribution from prison guards or officials.

Authorities permitted prisoners to register complaints with state and national human rights commissions, but the authority of the commissions extended only to recommending that authorities redress grievances. Government officials reportedly often failed to comply with a 2012 Supreme Court order instructing the central government and local authorities to conduct regular checks on police stations to monitor custodial violence.

In many states the NHRC made unannounced visits to state prisons, but NHRC jurisdiction does not extend to military detention centers. An NHRC special rapporteur visited state prisons to verify that authorities provided medical care to all inmates. The rapporteur visited prisons on a regular basis throughout the year but did not release a report to the public or the press.

d. Arbitrary Arrest or Detention

The law prohibits arbitrary arrest and detention, but both occurred during the year. Police also used special security laws to postpone judicial reviews of arrests. Pretrial detention was arbitrary and lengthy, sometimes exceeding the duration of the sentence given to those convicted.

According to human rights NGOs, some police used torture, mistreatment, and arbitrary detention to obtain forced or false confessions. In some cases police reportedly held suspects without registering their arrests and denied detainees sufficient food and water.

Role of the Police and Security Apparatus

The 29 states and seven union territories have primary responsibility for maintaining law and order, with policy oversight from the central government. Police are under state jurisdiction. The Ministry of Home Affairs controls most paramilitary forces, the internal intelligence bureaus, and national law enforcement agencies, and provides training for senior officials from state police forces.

According to Human Rights Watch, cases of arbitrary arrest, torture, and forced confessions by security forces remained common. Police forces continued to be overworked, underpaid, and subjected to political pressure, in some cases contributing to corruption.

The effectiveness of law enforcement and security forces varied widely throughout the country. According to the code of criminal procedure, Section 197, courts may not hear a case against a police officer unless the central or state government first authorizes prosecution. Nonetheless, NGOs reported that in many instances police refused to register victim's complaints, termed "first information reports" (FIR), on crimes reported against officers, effectively preventing victims from pursuing justice. In addition, NGOs reported that victims were sometimes reluctant to report crimes committed by police due to fear of retribution. There were cases of officers at all levels acting with impunity, but there were also cases of security officials held accountable for illegal actions. Military courts investigated cases of abuse by the armed forces and paramilitary forces. Authorities tried cases against law enforcement officers in public courts. Authorities sometimes transferred officers after convicting them of a crime.

The NHRC recommended the Criminal Investigations Department investigate all deaths taking place during police pursuits, arrests, or escape attempts. Many states did not follow this nonbinding recommendation and continued to conduct internal reviews at the discretion of senior officers.

While NHRC guidelines call for state governments to report all cases of deaths from police actions to the NHRC within 48 hours, state governments did not consistently adhere to those guidelines. The NHRC also called for state governments to provide monetary compensation to families of victims, but the state governments did not consistently adhere to this practice. Authorities did not require the armed forces to report custodial deaths to the NHRC.

On January 30, a video released by the Aam Aadmi Party allegedly showed three policemen in New Delhi beating students protesting the death of Dalit student Rohith Vemula. The protesters claimed their protest was peaceful and did not justify the treatment by the police or the subsequent charges.

On October 1, four persons died and nearly 30 were injured after police reportedly fired on protesting villagers in Hazaribagh District, Jharkhand. According to media reports, the villagers were protesting acquisition of land for the development of coal mines by the central government-owned National Thermal Power Corporation.

Arrest Procedures and Treatment of Detainees

Arbitrary Arrest: The code of criminal procedure prohibits arbitrary arrest or detention, but in some cases police reportedly continued to arrest citizens arbitrarily. There were reports of police detaining individuals for custodial interrogation without identifying themselves or providing arrest warrants.

Pretrial Detention: Authorities must promptly inform persons detained on criminal charges of the charges against them and of their right to legal counsel. Under the criminal code, a magistrate may authorize the detention of an accused person for a period of no more than 90 days prior to filing charges. Under standard criminal procedure, authorities must release the accused on bail after 90 days. The code also allows police to summon individuals for questioning, but it does not grant police prearrest investigative detention authority. There were incidents in which authorities allegedly detained suspects beyond legal limits.

There were reported cases in which police denied suspects the right to meet with legal counsel as well as cases in which police unlawfully monitored suspects' conversations and violated confidentiality rights. The constitution mandates that authorities provide defendants with "economic or other disabilities" free legal counsel, but authorities do not assess this need systematically. By law authorities must allow family members access to detainees, but this was not always observed. Arraignment of detainees must occur within 24 hours unless authorities hold the suspect under a preventive detention law. State authorities invoked preventive detention laws, most frequently in Delhi but also in the states of Gujarat, Maharashtra, Uttar Pradesh, Punjab, and Kashmir.

Police may detain an individual without charge for up to 30 days. The law also permits authorities to hold a detainee in judicial custody without charge for up to 180 days (including the 30 days in police custody). The UAPA, which gives authorities the ability to detain persons without charge in cases related to insurgency or terrorism, makes no bail provisions for foreign nationals, and allows courts to deny bail in the case of detained citizens. It presumes the accused to be guilty if the prosecution can produce evidence of the possession of arms or explosives, or the presence of fingerprints at a crime scene, regardless of whether authorities demonstrate criminal intent. State governments also reportedly held persons without bail for extended periods before filing formal charges under the UAPA.

The law permits preventive detention in certain cases. The National Security Act allows police to detain persons considered security risks anywhere in the country, except Jammu and Kashmir, without charge or trial for as long as one year. The law allows family members and lawyers to visit national security detainees and requires authorities to inform a detainee of the grounds for detention within five days, or 10 to 15 days in exceptional circumstances.

The Public Safety Act, which applies only in Jammu and Kashmir, permits state authorities to detain persons without charge or judicial review for up to two years without visitation from family members. Authorities allowed detainees access to a lawyer during interrogation, but police in Jammu and Kashmir allegedly routinely employed arbitrary detention and denied detainees access to lawyers and medical attention. According to media reports, approximately 440 individuals in Jammu and Kashmir have been detained without trial since the beginning of large-scale protests in July. Human rights activist Khurram Pervez was arrested and detained by security forces in September prior to his departure to address the UN Human Rights Council on the human rights situation in Jammu and Kashmir. On October 19, UN experts called on the government to release Pervez immediately. On November 30, authorities released Pervez after a court ruled his detention illegal.

The Human Rights Law Network (HRLN) in Kochi, Kerala, reported certain prisoners with mental disabilities in the Kerala central prison considered "not fit for trial" had awaited trial for 10 to 26 years. According to the NGO, the prisoners in some cases were in detention far longer than their potential sentences. In 2013 the HRLN filed a writ petition with the Kerala High Court for the release of those prisoners. The court responded by issuing an order directing the state government to provide adequate medical treatment to the accused to render them fit for trial. The case was pending in the Kerala High Court at year's end.

Lengthy arbitrary detention remained a significant problem due to overburdened and under resourced court systems and a lack of legal safeguards. The government continued efforts to reduce lengthy detentions and alleviate prison overcrowding by using "fast track" courts, which specified trial deadlines, provided directions for case management, and encouraged the use of bail. Some NGOs criticized these courts for failing to uphold due process and requiring detainees unable to afford bail remain in detention.

NCRB data showed most individuals awaiting trial spent more than three months in jail before they could secure bail, and nearly 65 percent spent between three months to five years before being released on bail.

e. Denial of Fair Public Trial

The law provides for an independent judiciary, but judicial corruption was widespread.

The judicial system remained seriously overburdened and lacked modern case management systems, often delaying or denying justice. According to 2015-16 data released by the Supreme Court, there was a 43 percent vacancy of judges in the country's 24 high courts as of October 1.

On April 25, after a 10-year investigation, the special Maharashtra Control of Organized Crime Act court in Mumbai acquitted nine Muslim defendants accused of bomb attacks in Malegaon, Maharashtra, in 2006 and 2008, which killed 31 and injured 312,The National Investigation Agency also filed charges against Hindu nationalists for perpetrating the same attacks. After investigations by three agencies--the Maharashtra Antiterrorism Squad, the Central Bureau of Investigation, and the National Investigation Agency--the court dismissed all terror charges due to lack of evidence.

Trial Procedures

The criminal procedure code provides for public trials, except in proceedings that involve official secrets or state security. Defendants enjoy the presumption of innocence, except as described under UAPA conditions, and may choose their counsel. The state provides free legal counsel to defendants who cannot afford it, but circumstances often limited access to competent counsel, and an overburdened justice system resulted in lengthy delays in court cases, with disposition sometimes taking more than a decade.

The law allows defendants access to relevant government evidence in most civil and criminal cases, but the government reserved the right to withhold information and did so in cases it considered sensitive. While defendants have the right to confront accusers and present their own witnesses and evidence, defendants sometimes did not exercise this right due to lack of proper legal representation. Defendants have the right not to testify or confess guilt. Courts must announce sentences publicly, and there are effective channels for appeal at most levels of the judicial system.

Political Prisoners and Detainees

There were reports of political prisoners and detainees. NGOs reported the Jammu and Kashmir government held political prisoners and between 2005 and 2014 temporarily detained more than 690 persons characterized as terrorists, insurgents, and separatists under the Public Safety Act. On July 20, a Kolkata court acquitted veteran Communist Party India (Maoist) spokesperson Gour Chakraborty, who was arrested in 2009 and charged with several offenses, including sedition. The court released Chakraborty after the prosecution failed to substantiate the charges.

Civil Judicial Procedures and Remedies

Individuals, or NGOs on behalf of individuals or groups, may file public interest litigation petitions in any high court or directly to the Supreme Court to seek judicial redress of public injury. Grievances can include a breach of public duty by a government agent or a violation of a provision of the constitution. NGOs credited public-interest litigation petitions with making government officials accountable to civil society organizations in cases involving allegations of corruption and partiality.

On January 13, the Bombay High Court addressed a two-fold rise in reported custodial death and police torture cases from 2014 to 2015 and directed the Maharashtra government to submit a report to the court. The court criticized the government for its failure to install closed-circuit television cameras in police stations, despite a court order.

f. Arbitrary or Unlawful Interference with Privacy, Family, Home, or Correspondence

While the constitution does not contain an explicit right to privacy, the Supreme Court has found such a right implicit in other constitutional provisions, most notably Article 21. The law, with some exceptions, prohibits arbitrary interference. The government generally respected this provision, although at times authorities infringed upon the privacy rights of citizens. The law requires police to obtain warrants to conduct searches and seizures, except in cases in which such actions would cause undue delay. Police must justify warrantless searches in writing to the nearest magistrate with jurisdiction over the offense.

The Official Secrets Act hindered transparency and accountability with regard to electronic surveillance. Responding to a query in the lower house of parliament in August, the Union Home Ministry stated the government set up an interministerial committee to examine the provisions of the Official Secrets Act and that the matter was under consideration.

Both the central and state governments intercepted communications under the authority of the Telegraph Act 1885, section 5(2), and under section 69 of the Information Technology Act 2000, as amended. The Group of Experts on Privacy convened in 2012 by the Government of India Planning Commission, the most recent review available, noted that the differences between these two statutes had created an unclear regulatory regime that was, according to the report, "inconsistent, nontransparent, prone to misuse, and does not provide remedy or compensation to aggrieved individuals."

The UAPA provides an additional legal basis for warrantless searches. The UAPA also allows use of evidence obtained from intercepted communications in terrorist cases. In Jammu and Kashmir, Punjab and Manipur, security officials have special authorities to search and arrest without a warrant.

The Chhattisgarh Special Public Security Act (CSPSA) of 2005 allows police to detain a person without charge for as long as 90 days. Opponents argued the law, which authorizes detention of individuals with a "tendency to pose an obstacle to the administration of law," infringed upon privacy and free speech. The government detained two journalists under the CSPSA, accusing them of complicity in a deadly attack on police by Naxalite insurgents; some media reports indicated authorities imprisoned the journalists because of their reporting. A local court acquitted one of the two journalists on July 21.

g. Abuses in Internal Conflict

The country's armed forces, the security forces of individual states, and paramilitary forces engaged in armed conflict with insurgent groups in several northeastern states, and with Maoist insurgents in the north, central, and eastern parts of the country--although the intensity of these conflicts continued to decrease significantly. Army and central security forces remained stationed at conflict areas in the northeast.

The use of force by all parties to the conflicts resulted in deaths and injuries to both conflict participants and civilians. There were reports government security forces committed extrajudicial killings, including staging encounter killings to conceal the deaths of captured militants. Human rights groups claimed police refused to release bodies in cases of alleged "encounters." Authorities did not require the armed forces to report custodial deaths to the NHRC.

The July 8 killing of Hizbul Mujahidden commander Burhan Wani led to continuing civilian protests in the Kashmir Valley and resulted in 90 deaths, including 88 civilians and two police officers. According to media reports, more than 4,500 civilians and more than 4,000 security personnel were injured. Schools, markets, offices, and businesses remained closed for extended periods.

The central and state governments and the armed forces investigated complaints and punished some violations committed by government forces. Authorities arrested and tried insurgents under terrorism-related legislation.

There were few investigations and prosecutions of human rights violations arising from internal conflicts. NGOs claimed that due to AFSPA immunity provisions, authorities did not hold the armed forces responsible for the deaths of civilians killed in Jammu and Kashmir in previous years.

Insurgents and terrorists reportedly committed attacks on roads and railways.

Killings: According to NGO and media reports, the apparently indiscriminate use of shotguns loaded with birdshot by security forces to control crowds, including violent protests, in Jammu and Kashmir resulted in 87 civilian deaths and blinded hundreds more, including children.

In Maoist-affected districts, there were reports of abuses by security forces and insurgents. On February 27, security forces killed Manda Kadraka, a member of an Odisha tribal community, during an exchange of gunfire with Maoists in Rayagada District. Police claimed Kadraka was a Maoist and died after exchanging fire with security forces. The Niyamgiri Surakhya Samithi, an organization that works for the welfare of the Dongria Kondh tribal group, maintained Kadraka was not a combatant and that the police killed him to suppress protests against mining in the surrounding area. In July, 10 soldiers were killed in an attack by Maoist insurgents in the Dumrinala area, 100 miles outside Patna, the capital of Bihar. According to state police officials, the insurgents employed improvised explosive devices and small arms in the attack on soldiers.

<u>Abductions</u>: Human rights groups maintained military, paramilitary, and insurgent forces abducted numerous persons in Manipur, Jharkhand, and the Maoist belt. Human rights activists alleged cases of prisoners tortured or killed during detention. During the year media outlets reported cases of abduction by insurgent groups in Manipur. On June 28, the Assam Rifles disrupted a plot by the People's Revolutionary Party of Kangleipak insurgent group to abduct and extort petroleum truck drivers. Contractors working on a railway project connecting Manipur's capital Imphal to Jiribam also reported abduction and extortion threats by militant groups. In April police recovered the body of a driver from Lhangnom village in Manipur's Senapati District. The driver was allegedly abducted by insurgents on March 3.

<u>Physical Abuse, Punishment, and Torture</u>: There were reports government security forces tortured, raped, and mistreated insurgents and alleged terrorists in custody and injured demonstrators. All parties to the conflicts injured civilians.

<u>Child Soldiers</u>: Insurgent groups reportedly used children to attack government entities in roles such as bomb couriers. The Ministry of Home Affairs reported Maoist groups conscripted boys and girls ages six to 12 into specific children's units (Bal Dasta and Bal Sangham) in Bihar, Jharkhand, Chhattisgarh, and Odisha States. The Maoist groups used the children in combat and intelligence-gathering roles. Insurgents trained children as spies and couriers, as well as in the use of arms, planting explosives, and intelligence gathering. NGOs in Manipur reported the National Socialist Council of Nagaland Isak-Muivah (NSCN-IM) recruited nearly 3,000 personnel, a large percentage of whom were minors, between January and April. Security officials in Manipur corroborated the trend.

Although the United Nations was not able to verify all allegations, reports submitted to parliament contained similar allegations. Recruitment of children by Maoist armed groups allegedly continued. Observers reported children as young as 12 were members of Maoist youth groups and allied militia. They reportedly handled weapons and improvised explosive devices. Maoists reportedly held children against their will and threatened severe reprisals, including the killing of family members, if the children attempted to escape. There were reports of girls serving in Maoist groups. The government claimed, based on statements of several women formerly associated with Maoist groups, that sexual violence, including rape and other forms of abuse, was a practice in some Maoist camps.

According to government sources, Maoist armed groups used children as human shields in confrontations with security forces. Attacks on schools by Maoists continued to affect children's access to education in affected areas. There were continued reports on the use of schools as military barracks and bases. The deployment of government security forces near schools remained a concern. There were reports armed groups recruited children from schools in Chhattisgarh.

Other Conflict-related Abuse: As of July the Internal Displacement Monitoring Center estimated conflicts and instability in the country displaced 3.7 million persons.

Tens of thousands of Kashmiri Pandits (Hindus) have fled the Kashmir Valley to Jammu, Delhi, and other areas in the country since 1990 because of conflict and violent intimidation, including destruction of houses of worship, sexual abuse, and theft of property, by Kashmiri separatists. The Kashmiri Pandits began to leave Kashmir after the 1990 onset of insurgency against the Indian state. In Jammu and Kashmir, central government assistance to displaced Kashmiri Pandits consisted of monthly cash allowances and food rations, but some members of the group claimed the assistance failed to address their livelihood needs. In May 2015 thousands of Kashmiri Pandits and members of the National Conference protested against state government plans to resettle the group in secluded enclaves in Kashmir without consultation.

In the central and eastern areas, armed conflicts between Maoist insurgents and government security forces over land and mineral resources in tribal forest areas continued, affecting 182 of the country's 626 districts in 20 of its 29 states. Human rights advocates alleged the government's operations sought not only to suppress the Maoists but also to force tribal persons off their land, allowing for commercial exploitation.

Internally displaced person (IDP) camps continued to operate in Chhattisgarh for tribal persons displaced during the 2005 fighting between Maoists and state-sponsored militia Salwa Judum.

Throughout the year there were reports by media organizations and academic institutions of corporations' human rights abuses against tea workers, including violations of the Plantation Labor Act. In some cases violent strikes resulted from companies withholding medical care required by law. Other reports indicated workers had difficulty accessing clean water, with open sewage flowing through company housing areas. The tea industry is among the largest private-sector employers in the country, providing work for more than one million permanent workers and up to two million seasonal laborers.

Between January 11 and 14, tribal women alleged rape and sexual assault by security forces during search operations in Nendra, Chhattisgarh. Six tribal women from the village of Kunna alleged security forces assaulted them on January 12. On January 25, Amnesty International called for an investigation of police inaction in 13 sexual assault cases of tribal women in Nendra village. In April the National Commission for Scheduled Tribes (NCST) claimed mass sexual abuse by security forces during counterinsurgency operations. The NCST recommended that investigation of three specific cases be transferred from district police authorities to the state's Criminal Investigation Department.

Section 2. Respect for Civil Liberties, Including:

a. Freedom of Speech and Press

The constitution provides for freedom of speech and expression, but it does not explicitly mention freedom of the press. The government generally respected these rights.

<u>Freedom of Speech and Expression</u>: Individuals routinely criticized the government publicly and privately. According to Human Rights Watch, however, sedition and criminal defamation laws were used to prosecute citizens who criticize government officials or oppose state policies. In certain cases local authorities arrested individuals under laws against hate speech for expressions of political views.

On February 12, Delhi police arrested Jawaharlal Nehru University students' union president Kanhaiya Kumar and seven other students, charging them with sedition for allegedly shouting "anti-India" slogans at a February 9 protest. The arrests and subsequent administrative disciplinary measures resulted in protests on other university campuses. According to the NHRC, Kumar was "abused and physically assaulted" at court when he appeared for a bail hearing on February 17. In March the Delhi High Court released Kumar and two other students on bail, which was extended to August 26. On September 6, the Delhi High Court extended bail and enjoined the university administration from taking administrative action against Kumar until the next hearing.

On September 5, the Supreme Court stated the government could not bring charges of sedition against a person for criticizing the government or its policies. This ruling was in response to a petition filed by NGO Common Cause to curb the use of sedition provisions under the Indian Penal Code to restrict speech.

<u>Press and Media Freedoms</u>: Independent media generally expressed a wide variety of views without restriction. The law prohibits content that could harm religious sentiments or provoke enmity among groups, and authorities invoked these laws to restrict print media, broadcast media, and publication or distribution of books.

On March 21, the Chhattisgarh police arrested journalist Prabhat Singh in Dantewada for allegedly sharing a message critical of the state police on a messaging application and charged him under the Information Technology Act. On March 26, Chhattisgarh police arrested journalist Deepak Jaiswal for inquiring about the Prabhat Singh case. A court granted Jaiswal bail on June 6, and the Chhattisgarh High Court granted Prabhat Singh bail on June 22.

The government maintained a monopoly on AM radio stations and restricted FM radio licenses for entertainment and educational content. Widely distributed private satellite television provided competition for Doordarshan, the government-owned television network. State governments banned the import or sale of some books due to material government censors deemed inflammatory or could provoke communal or religious tensions.

<u>Violence and Harassment</u>: Some journalists and media persons reportedly experienced violence and harassment in response to their reporting. In February Asianet News channel anchor Sindhu Sooryakumar reportedly received more than 2,000 abusive calls and death threats after moderating a debate on Hinduism. On February 28, police arrested five persons in connection with these threats.

<u>Censorship or Content Restrictions</u>: In August 2015 the Central Board of Film Certification (CBFC) in Chennai refused to certify the film Muttrupulliya, which portrays Tamil life in post-war Sri Lanka, over concerns the film glorified the war. In September 2015 the filmmakers appealed the CBFC refusal before the Film Certification Appellate Tribunal. In March the filmmakers won the appeal, and the CBFC lifted the ban on the film.

<u>Libel/Slander Laws</u>: In July the Supreme Court reviewed an appeal from a Tamil Nadu trial court filed by politician Vijaykanth, challenging the constitutionality of a law permitting prosecutors to file defamation cases on behalf of public servants.

The court also ordered the state government to provide a list of criminal defamation cases brought on behalf of then chief minister Jayalalithaa by Tamil Nadu prosecutors. According to media reports, the list submitted by the Tamil Nadu government on August 17 included 213 cases filed from May 2011 through July 2016.

<u>National Security</u>: In some cases government authorities cited laws protecting national interest to restrict media content.

On June 9, Sakshi TV was taken off the air in Andhra Pradesh until June 22, after it publicized the hunger strike of Kapu caste leader Mudragada Padmanabham. Deputy Chief Minister N. Chinarajappa stated the channel would remain off-air as long as the hunger strike continued, since covering the protest could potentially disturb law and order in the state.

In July the Jammu and Kashmir government reportedly raided local printing presses, stopped publication, and detained press staff while enforcing a news blackout during a period of unrest. In addition to restrictions on newspaper publication, internet and cellular communication was also heavily restricted.

<u>Nongovernmental Impact</u>: In a statement released on June 16, UN Special rapporteurs on human rights expressed the view that FCRA Foreign Contribution Regulation Act (FCRA) "provisions were increasingly being used…to silence organizations involved in advocating civil, political, economic, social, environmental, or cultural priorities, which may differ from those backed by the Government." The statement highlighted the suspension of foreign banking licenses for NGOs including Greenpeace India, Lawyers Collective, and the Sabrang Trust.

Internet Freedom

There were some government restrictions on access to the internet, disruptions of access to the internet, and censorship of online content. There were also reports the government occasionally monitored users of digital media, such as chat rooms and person-to-person communications. The IT Act permits the government to block internet sites and content and criminalizes sending messages the government deems inflammatory or offensive. Both central and state governments have the power to issue directions for blocking, intercepting, monitoring, or decrypting computer information.

In 2015 the Supreme Court struck down section 66A of the IT Act, which had resulted in a significant number of arrests between 2012 and 2015 for content published on social media. According to NCRB data, police made 3,137 arrests under 66A in 2015, compared with 2,423 arrests in 2014. As of January 1, 575 individuals remained incarcerated under all sections of the IT act. The Supreme Court upheld other provisions of the act authorizing the government to block certain online content. Under section 69A of the act, the government can still order content blocks without court approval.

The central monitoring system (CMS), which began pilot operations in 2013, continued to allow governmental agencies to monitor electronic communications in real time without informing the subject or a judge. The CMS is a mass electronic surveillance data-mining program installed by the Center for Development of Telematics, a government-owned telecommunications technology development center. The CMS gives security agencies and income tax officials centralized access to the telecommunication network and the ability to hear and record mobile, landline, and satellite telephone calls and Voice over Internet Protocol, to read private e-mails and mobile texts, and to track geographical locations of individuals in real time. Authorities can also use it to monitor posts shared on social media and track users' search histories on Google, without oversight by courts or parliament. This monitoring facility was available to nine security agencies, including the Intelligence Bureau, the Research and Analysis Wing, and the Home Affairs Ministry. In May 2015 former communications minister Milind Deora expressed concern that without comprehensive privacy laws, the system was not sufficiently accountable and could impinge on freedom of speech.

Freedom House, a civil liberty organization, released a report in October 2015 rating the country "partly free" with respect to internet user rights, including accessibility, limits on content, and violations of individual's rights. The NGO reported the government decreased the number of incidents concerning connectivity, restricted access, and documented incidents of physical attacks on internet users for content posted online. According to the report, key internet controls that existed between May 2014 and May 2015 included blocking of political, social, and religious content. The report cited the CMS as a potential internet freedom concern.

Government regulations on internet content prohibit many types of material including "harmful" and "insulting" content. Authorities may hold search engines liable for displaying prohibited content. Authorities require cyber cafes to install surveillance cameras and provide the government with records of user browsing activity.

On January 6, media reported 24-year-old Anwar Sadiq of Malappuram in Kerala was charged with sedition for social media comments he allegedly made about a military officer killed during a counterterror operation at Pathankot Air Force Base.

On March 25, two students from a town in Puttur, Karnataka, were arrested and later released for posting "Pakistan Ki Jai" (Hail Pakistan) on a phone messaging application during the India-Pakistan World T20 cricket match, according to media reports.

The government requested user data from internet companies. According to Facebook's January 2016 transparency report for the second half of 2015, the government made 5,561 requests. Facebook complied with 51 percent of those requests. Google also highlighted in its most recent transparency report an increase in government requests to share user data.

According to industry experts, approximately 35 percent of the population had access to the internet in 2016.

Academic Freedom and Cultural Events

In rare cases the government applied restrictions to the travel and activities of visiting experts and scholars; however, in most cases the government supported and issued visas for international academic conferences and exchanges.

b. Freedom of Peaceful Assembly and Association

The law provides for the freedoms of assembly and association, and the government generally respected those rights.

Freedom of Assembly

The law provides for freedom of assembly. Authorities often required permits and notification before parades or demonstrations, and local governments generally respected the right to protest peacefully, except in Jammu and Kashmir, where the state government sometimes denied permits to separatist political parties for public gatherings, and security forces sometimes reportedly detained and assaulted members of political groups engaged in peaceful protest (see section 1.g.). During periods of civil unrest in Jammu and Kashmir, authorities used the criminal procedure code to ban public assemblies or impose a curfew.

Security forces, including local police, often disrupted demonstrations and used excessive force when attempting to disperse protesters.

On March 22, following the suicide of Dalit doctoral student Rohith Vemula, police responded to protests by teachers and students against the University of Hyderabad administration. Students and human rights NGOs alleged the police used disproportionate force. Two teachers and 36 students were detained.

There were restrictions on the organization of international conferences. Authorities required NGOs to secure approval from the Ministry of Home Affairs before organizing international conferences. Authorities routinely granted permission, although in some cases the approval process was lengthy. Some human rights groups claimed this practice provided the government with tacit control over the work of NGOs and constituted a restriction on freedom of assembly and association.

Freedom of Association

The law provides for freedom of association. While the government generally respected that right, the government's increased regulation of NGO activities that receive foreign funding has caused concern. In certain cases, for example, the government required "prior approval" of some NGOs foreign funds, and in other instances declined to renew NGOs' FCRA registration.

NGOs expressed continued concern regarding the government's enforcement of FCRA, provisions of which bar some foreign-funded NGOs from engaging in activities the government believed were not in the "national or public interest," curtailing the work of some civil society organizations. Some NGOs expressed concern over politically motivated enforcement of the act to intimidate organizations that address social issues or criticize the government or its policies, arguing that the law's use of broad and vague terms such as "public interest" and "national interest" have left it open to abuse. Some multi-national and domestic companies also stated that in some instances the act made it difficult to comply with government-mandated corporate social responsibility obligations due to lengthy and complicated registration processes.

According to media reports, in early November the Ministry of Home Affairs rejected FCRA registration renewals of 25 NGOs, including Lawyer's Collective and Compassion International's two primary partners. In addition, some NGOs were placed on a "prior permissions" list, which requires government preapproval of any transfer of funds from abroad. Several NGOs stated these actions threaten their ability to continue to operate in the country.

In April the UN special rapporteur on freedom of assembly and association published a legal analysis asserting that the FCRA did not conform to international law, principles, and standards. In June the UN special rapporteurs on human rights defenders, on freedom of expression, and on freedom of association called on the government to repeal the FCRA.

According to media reports, the government took action to suspend foreign banking licenses or freeze accounts for NGOs on the basis that they received foreign funding without the proper clearances or illegally combined foreign and domestic funding streams, although some human rights organizations reported these types of actions were sometimes used to target specific NGOs.

c. Freedom of Religion

See the Department of State's *International Religious Freedom Report* at www.state.gov/religiousfreedomreport/.

d. Freedom of Movement, Internally Displaced Persons, Protection of Refugees, and Stateless Persons

The law provides for freedom of internal movement, foreign travel, emigration, and repatriation. The government generally respected these rights. In August 2015 the implementation of a land boundary agreement between India and Bangladesh enfranchised more than 50,000 previously stateless residents, providing access to education and health services.

The government generally cooperated with the Office of the UN High Commissioner for Refugees (UNHCR) and other humanitarian organizations in providing protection and assistance to some IDPs, refugees, returning refugees, asylum seekers, stateless persons, and other persons of concern. The government generally allowed UNHCR to assist only those asylum seekers and refugees from noncontiguous countries. The country hosted a large refugee population, including 110,000 Tibetan refugees, notably the Dalai Lama.

<u>In-country Movement</u>: The central government relaxed restrictions on travel by foreigners to Arunachal Pradesh, Nagaland, Mizoram, Manipur, and parts of Jammu and Kashmir, excluding foreign nationals from Pakistan, China, and Burma. The Ministry of Home Affairs and state governments required citizens to obtain special permits upon arrival when traveling to certain restricted areas.

Security forces often searched and questioned travelers at vehicle checkpoints in areas of the Kashmir Valley and before public events in New Delhi, or after major terrorist attacks.

<u>Foreign Travel</u>: The government may legally deny a passport to any applicant for engaging in activities outside the country "prejudicial to the sovereignty and integrity of the nation."

Citizens from Jammu and Kashmir faced extended delays, sometimes up to two years, for issuance or renewal of passports. The government reportedly subjected applicants born in Jammu and Kashmir, including children born to military officers deployed in the state, to additional scrutiny and police clearances before issuing them passports.

Internally Displaced Persons

Authorities located IDP settlements throughout the country, including those containing groups displaced by internal armed conflicts in Jammu and Kashmir, the Maoist belt, the northeastern states (see section 1.g.), and Gujarat. According to International Displacement Monitoring Center (IDMC) statistics from December 31, 2015, longstanding regional conflicts had displaced at least 612,000 persons. Estimating the exact number of those displaced by conflict or violence was difficult, because no central government agency was responsible for monitoring the movements of displaced persons, and humanitarian and human rights agencies had limited access to camps and affected regions. While authorities registered residents of IDP camps, an unknown number of displaced persons resided outside camps. Many IDPs lacked sufficient food, clean water, shelter, and health care (see additional reporting on IDPs in section 1.g.).

Paramilitary operations against Maoists displaced members of the Gutti Koya tribe in the Dandakaranya forests in Chhattisgarh, who migrated to the neighboring Khammam and Warangal districts in Telangana. Following bifurcation of Andhra Pradesh to form the new state of Telangana in 2014, the state governments transferred parts of Khammam District with Gutti Koya settlements to Andhra Pradesh.

The IDMC estimated the number of IDPs in Chhattisgarh at 50,000, in Telangana at 13,820, and in Andhra Pradesh at 6,240. The Chhattisgarh government reportedly did not acknowledge IDPs in Andhra Pradesh camps as Chhattisgarh residents, and the Andhra Pradesh government reportedly provided them little support. Repatriation of IDPs was difficult due to development projects on Adivasi forestland and rural-urban migration trends.

National policy or legislation did not address the issue of internal displacement resulting from armed conflict or from ethnic or communal violence. Responsibility for the welfare of IDPs was generally the purview of state governments and local authorities, allowing for gaps in services and poor accountability. The central government provided limited assistance to IDPs. IDPs had access to NGOs and human rights organizations, but neither access nor assistance was standard for all IDPs or all situations.

Protection of Refugees

The 1946 Foreigners Act does not contain the term "refugee," treating refugees as any other foreigners. Undocumented physical presence in the country is a criminal offense. Refugees without documentation were vulnerable to forced repatriation and reportedly to abuse. The government generally provided protection against the expulsion or return of refugees to countries where refugees would face threats to their safety or freedom due to race, religion, nationality, membership in a particular social group, or political opinion.

Access to Asylum: Absent a legal framework, the government sometimes granted asylum on a situational basis on humanitarian grounds in accordance with international law. This approach resulted in varying standards of protection for different refugee and asylum seeker groups. The government recognized refugees from Tibet and Sri Lanka and honored UNHCR decisions on refugee status determination for individuals from other countries.

UNHCR did not maintain an official presence in the country, but the government permitted UNHCR staff access to refugees in urban centers and allowed it to operate in Tamil Nadu to assist with Sri Lankan refugee repatriation. UNHCR registered asylum seekers and conducted refugee status determination for refugees from noncontiguous countries and Burma. Authorities did not permit UNHCR direct access to Sri Lankan refugee camps, Tibetan settlements, or asylum seekers in Mizoram; but it permitted asylum seekers from Mizoram to travel to New Delhi to meet UNHCR officials. UNHCR did not have access to asylum seekers in Mizoram. The government generally permitted NGOs, international humanitarian organizations, and foreign governments access to Sri Lankan refugee camps and Tibetan settlements but generally denied access to asylum seekers in Mizoram. UNHCR estimated registration of 6,870 Rohingya and 6,855 Chin from Burma in New Delhi and estimated tens of thousands of additional asylum seekers remained unregistered.

According to Chin Human Rights Organization (CHRO) activists in Mizoram, some Chins living in Mizoram returned to Burma after the installation of the new government in that country. Faced with falling numbers, CHRO and its affiliates reduced their scale of operations in Mizoram.

After the end of the Sri Lankan civil war, the government ceased registering Sri Lankans as refugees. The Tamil Nadu government assisted UNHCR by providing exit permission for Sri Lankan refugees to repatriate voluntarily.

The benefits provided to Sri Lankan Tamil refugees by the state government of Tamil Nadu were applicable only within Tamil Nadu.

Refugees outside Delhi faced added expense and time to register their asylum claims.

Refugee Abuse: The government did not target refugees for harassment, and police and courts appropriately protected refugees. Refugees, however, reported exploitation by nongovernment actors, including assaults, gender-based violence, frauds, and labor exploitation.

Problems of domestic violence, sexual abuse, and early and forced marriage continued. Gender-based violence and sexual abuse was common in camps for Sri Lankans. Many urban refugees worked in the informal sector or in occupations such as street vending, where they suffered from police extortion, nonpayment of wages, and exploitation.

Employment: The government granted work authorization to many UNHCR-registered refugees, and others found employment in the informal sector. Some refugees reported discrimination by employers.

<u>Access to Basic Services</u>: Although the country generally allowed recognized refugees and asylum seekers access to housing, primary and secondary education, health care, and the courts, access varied by state and by population. Refugees were able to access public services. In most cases where refugees were denied access, it was due to a lack of knowledge on refugee rights by the service provider. In many cases UNHCR was able to intervene successfully and advocate for refugee access. In 2012 the government began allowing UNHCR-registered refugees and asylum seekers to apply for long-term visas that would provide work authorization and access to higher education. For undocumented asylum seekers, UNHCR provided a letter upon registration indicating the person was under consideration for UNHCR mandate refugee status.

The 80,000 to 100,000 Burmese Chin asylum seekers in Mizoram generally reported adequate access to housing, education, and health services. Because most Chin asylum seekers lacked legal status and were unable to work legally, they were often unable to meet basic needs and remained vulnerable to abuse, discrimination, and harassment.

During the year several NGOs working with Rohingya refugees in Haryana complained of difficulties in enrolling Rohingya children without state-issued identification cards in government schools. Local school officials claimed all refugee children were welcome with a state-issued identity certificate.

The government did not fully fulfill a 2012 Ministry of Home Affairs directive to issue long-term visas to Rohingya. These visas would allow refugees to access formal employment in addition to education, health services, and bank accounts.

Government services such as mother-child health programs were available. Refugees were able to request protection from the police and courts as needed.

Sri Lankan refugees were permitted to work in Tamil Nadu. Police, however, reportedly summoned refugees back into the camps on short notice, particularly during sensitive political times such as elections, and required refugees or asylum seekers to remain in the camps for several days.

The government did not accept refugees for resettlement from other countries.

Stateless Persons

By law parents confer citizenship, and birth in the country does not automatically result in citizenship. Any person born in the country on or after January 26, 1950, but before July 1, 1987, obtained Indian citizenship by birth. A child born in the country on or after July 1, 1987, obtained citizenship if either parent was an Indian citizen at the time of the child's birth. Authorities considered those born in the country on or after December 3, 2004, citizens only if at least one parent was a citizen and the other was not illegally present in the country at the time of the child's birth. Authorities considered persons born outside the country on or after December 10, 1992, citizens if either parent was a citizen at the time of birth, but authorities did not consider those born outside the country after December 3, 2004, citizens unless their birth was registered at an Indian consulate within one year of the date of birth. Authorities could also confer citizenship through registration under specific categories and via naturalization after residing in the country for 12 years. Tibetans reportedly sometimes faced difficulty acquiring citizenship despite meeting the legal requirements.

According to UNHCR and NGOs, the country had a large population of stateless persons, but there were no reliable estimates of the number. Stateless populations included Chakmas and Hajongs, who entered the country decades ago from present-day Bangladesh, and groups affected by the 1947 partition of the subcontinent into India and Pakistan.

Kolkata-based Mahanirban Calcutta Research Group estimated the presence of approximately 45,000 unregistered Rohingyas in addition to those registered with UNHCR.

Approximately 70,000 stateless Bangladeshi Chakma persons lived in Arunachal Pradesh. On September 20, the Supreme Court ordered the central government and the Arunachal Pradesh state government to consider citizenship for Chakma and Hajong refugees who have lived in the state for almost 50 years. In the early 1960s, Buddhist Chakmas and Hajongs fled persecution from former East Pakistan (Bangladesh) and approximately 15,000 settled in the Changlang District of Arunachal Pradesh.

In May the Mizoram State government, which had previously refused to accept the repatriation of Bru refugees, submitted a plan to the Ministry of Home Affairs to repatriate more than 20,000 Brus, including 11,500 minors. Bru IDPs were lodged in six relief camps in North Tripura District. The ministry approved the Mizoram plan in July.

Children born in Sri Lankan refugee camps received Indian birth certificates. While Indian birth certificates alone do not entitle refugees to Indian citizenship, refugees may present Indian birth certificates to the Sri Lankan High Commission to commence registration as Sri Lankan citizens. Approximately 16,000 of 27,000 Sri Lankan refugee children born in the refugee camps have presented birth certificates to the Sri Lankan High Commission in Chennai.

UNHCR and refugee advocacy groups estimated that between 25,000 and 28,000 of the approximately 100,000 Sri Lankan Tamil refugees living in Tamil Nadu were "hill country" Tamils. While Sri Lankan law allows "hill country" refugees to present affidavits to secure Sri Lankan citizenship, UNHCR believed that until the Sri Lankan government processes their paperwork, authorities may consider such refugees potentially stateless.

Section 3. Freedom to Participate in the Political Process

The constitution provides citizens the ability to choose their government through free and fair periodic elections held by secret ballot and based on universal and equal suffrage.

Elections and Political Participation

Recent Elections: Voters elected President Pranab Mukherjee in 2012 to a five-year term, and Narendra Modi became prime minister following the victory of the National Democratic Alliance coalition led by the Bharatiya Janata Party in the May 2014 general elections. Observers considered these elections, which included more than 551 million participants, free and fair, despite isolated instances of violence.

The Election Commission of India is an independent constitutional body responsible for administering all elections at the central and state level throughout the country. International organizations reported fair and effective oversight by the commission during the April assembly elections in Assam, and May elections in West Bengal, Kerala, Tamil Nadu, and the Union Territory of Puducherry.

The Election Commission seized approximately one billion rupees ($15 million) in cash from various parts of Tamil Nadu in advance of the Legislative Assembly elections. The commission deferred voting in Aravakurichi and Thanjavur assembly districts following seizure of more than 60 million rupees ($902,000) in cash and other gifts.

<u>Political Parties and Political Participation</u>: The constitution provides for universal voting rights for all citizens age 18 and above. There were no restrictions placed on the formation of political parties or on individuals of any communities from participating in the election process. The election law bans the use of government resources for political campaigning and the Election Commission effectively enforced the law. The commission's guidelines ban opinion polls 48 hours prior to an election and cannot release results of exit polls until completion of the last phase (in a multiphase election).

<u>Participation of Women and Minorities</u>: The law reserves one-third of the seats in local councils for women. Religious, cultural, and traditional practices and ideas prevented women from proportional participation in political office. Nonetheless, women held many high-level political offices, including positions as ministers, members of parliament, and state chief ministers.

The constitution stipulates that to protect historically marginalized groups and provide for representation in the lower house of parliament, each state must reserve seats for Scheduled Castes and Scheduled Tribes in proportion to their population in the state. Only candidates belonging to these groups may contest elections in reserved constituencies. Members of minority populations served as prime minister, vice president, cabinet ministers, Supreme Court justices, and members of parliament.

Some Christians and Muslims were identified as Dalits, but the government limited reservations for Dalits to Hindus, Sikhs, and Jains.

Section 4. Corruption and Lack of Transparency in Government

The law provides criminal penalties for corruption by officials at all levels of government. Officials frequently engaged, however, in corrupt practices with impunity. There were numerous reports of government corruption during the year.

<u>Corruption</u>: Corruption was present at all levels of government. The CBI registered 237 cases of corruption between January and June. The commission operated a public hotline and a web portal. NGOs reported the payment of bribes to expedite services, such as police protection, school admission, water supply, or government assistance. Civil society organizations drew public attention to corruption throughout the year, including through demonstrations and websites that featured stories of corruption.

Media reports, NGOs, and activists reported links between contractors, militant groups, and security forces in infrastructure projects, narcotics trafficking, and timber smuggling in the northeastern states. These reports alleged ties among politicians, bureaucrats, security personnel, and insurgent groups. In Manipur and Nagaland, allegations of bribes paid to secure state government jobs were prevalent, especially in police and education departments.

Corruption sometimes hampered government programs to investigate allegations of government corruption. In July 2015 a Special Investigation Team (SIT) alleged officials from Lokayukta, an anticorruption statutory body, exchanged bribes for protection from potential corruption raids in Karnataka and arrested 10 individuals, including local officials. In response the Karnataka government amended the Lokayukta Act to allow for the removal of anticorruption officials. Corruption ombudsman Justice Bhaskar Rao resigned in December 2015. On August 4, the SIT charged Justice Rao with abetting conspiracy and corruption-related activities.

In July 2015 the Supreme Court ordered the CBI to take over a Madhya Pradesh state government investigation of fraud within the Professional Examination Board (Vyapam), a state government body that conducts school entrance and government service exams. Arrests in the case since the investigation began in 2013 included more than 2,000 individuals. In August the CBI registered a complaint against 60 individuals and filed charges against a student candidate and an impersonator. The Madhya Pradesh High Court granted bail to some of the accused. The CBI was also investigating the deaths of 48 individuals over the span of five years, including a journalist, who reported on the fraud.

On June 4, the Maharashtra agriculture and revenue minister, Eknath Khadse, resigned following allegations of corruption in a land deal involving his wife and son-in-law. On June 5, the Maharashtra chief minister, Devendra Fadnav, appointed a retired high court judge to investigate the corruption allegations.

Financial Disclosure: The law mandates asset declarations for all officers in the Indian Administrative Services. Both the Election Commission and the Supreme Court upheld mandatory disclosure of criminal and financial records for election candidates.

Public Access to Information: The law provides for public access to information. Although the government was often slow to respond to requests, the public could access personal documentation, city plans, and other public records through the Right to Information (RTI) online portal. RTI requests are limited to Indian citizens. The government charged a fee of 11 rupees (16 cents) per request. Citizens may appeal request denials to the Central Information Commission and then to the appropriate high court. Activists expressed concern that public authorities were sometimes unable to implement the RTI Act adequately and that rural inhabitants were not always aware of their rights under the act. Other activists credited the RTI act for increasing transparency, noting it was used to expose corrupt activities across the country. In May media reported the removal of a chapter in textbooks for Rajasthan middle school students related to the right to information across the country.

Section 5. Governmental Attitude Regarding International and Nongovernmental Investigation of Alleged Violations of Human Rights

Most domestic and international human rights groups generally operated without government restriction, investigating and publishing their findings on human rights cases. In some circumstances groups faced restrictions. Government officials were generally responsive to NGO requests. There were more than three million NGOs in the country advocating for social justice, sustainable development, and human rights. The government generally met with domestic NGOs, responded to their inquiries, and took action in response to their reports or recommendations. The NHRC worked cooperatively with numerous NGOs. Several NHRC committees had NGO representation. Human rights monitors in Jammu and Kashmir were able to document human rights violations, but security forces, police, and counterinsurgents at times reportedly restrained or harassed them.

Representatives of certain international human rights NGOs sometimes faced difficulties obtaining visas and reported that occasional official harassment and restrictions limited their public distribution of materials.

Police charged activists Teesta Setalvad, Javed Anand, Salim Sandhi, Feroz Gulzar, Mohammed Pathan, and Tanvir Jafri with embezzlement after donors claimed Setalvad, founder of Citizens for Justice and Peace (CJP) misused 1.5 million rupees ($22,500) collected to build a memorial to victims of the 2002 Gujarat riots. The Supreme Court granted defendants anticipatory bail after several denials in lower courts in Gujarat. The Gujarat state government froze CJP bank accounts in January 2014 pending the investigation. On August 17, the Supreme Court formally notified the Gujarat government it was seeking a response on a CJP appeal.

In July 2015 the CBI launched a second investigation of Setalvad and Anand for alleged misuse of grants from foreign donors. On March 9, the Supreme Court extended the interim bail to Setalvad and Anand. The activists alleged authorities filed the case in retaliation for their work on behalf of the victims in the Gujarat 2002 riots.

The United Nations or Other International Bodies: The government continued to restrict access by the United Nations to the northeastern states and Maoist-controlled areas. On August 17, UN High Commissioner for Human Rights Zeid Ra'ad Al Hussein expressed regret at the failure of government authorities to grant UNHCR access to Jammu and Kashmir given "grave concerns about recent allegations of serious human rights violations."

Government Human Rights Bodies: The NHRC is an independent and impartial investigatory and advisory body, established by the central government, with a dual mandate to investigate and remedy instances of human rights violations and to promote public awareness of human rights. It is directly accountable to parliament but works in close coordination with the Ministry of Home Affairs and the Ministry of Law and Justice. It has a mandate to address official violations of human rights or negligence in the prevention of violations, intervene in judicial proceedings involving allegations of human rights violations, and review any factors (including acts of terrorism) that infringe on human rights. The law authorizes the NHRC to issue summonses and compel testimony, produce documentation, and requisition public records. The NHRC also recommends appropriate remedies for abuses in the form of compensation to the victims of government killings or their families. It has neither the authority to enforce the implementation of its recommendations nor the power to address allegations against military and paramilitary personnel.

Human rights groups claimed these limitations hampered the work of the NHRC. While the NHRC has the authority to initiate investigations and to request state governments submit reports, it has no ability to enforce these requests, press charges, or grant compensation. It cannot investigate human rights violations by the armed forces. Some human rights NGOs criticized the NHRC's budgetary dependence on the government and its policy of not investigating abuses more than one year old. Some claimed the NHRC did not register all complaints, dismissed cases arbitrarily, did not investigate cases thoroughly, rerouted complaints back to the alleged violator, and did not adequately protect complainants.

Twenty-three of 29 states have human rights commissions, which operated independently under the auspices of the NHRC. In seven states the position of chairperson remained vacant. Some human rights groups alleged local politics influenced state committees, which were less likely to offer fair judgments than the NHRC.

In the course of its nationwide evaluation of state human rights committees, the HRLN observed most state committees had few or no minority, civil society, or female representatives. The HRLN claimed the committees were ineffective and at times hostile toward victims, hampered by political appointments, understaffed, and underfunded.

The Jammu and Kashmir commission does not have the authority to investigate alleged human rights violations committed by members of paramilitary security forces. The NHRC has jurisdiction over all human rights violations, except in certain cases involving the army. The NHRC has authority to investigate cases of human rights violations committed by Ministry of Home Affairs paramilitary forces operating under the AFSPA in the northeast states and in Jammu and Kashmir.

Section 6. Discrimination, Societal Abuses, and Trafficking in Persons

Women

Rape and Domestic Violence: The law criminalizes rape, except spousal rape when the woman is over the age of 15. Punishment ranges from prison terms of two years to life in prison, a fine of 20,418 rupees ($306), or both. Official statistics pointed to rape as the country's fastest growing crime, prompted by the increasing willingness of victims to report rapes, although observers believed the number of rapes remained underreported. Law enforcement and legal recourse for rape victims was inadequate, overtaxed, and unable to address the problem effectively. Police officers sometimes worked to reconcile rape victims and their attackers, in some cases encouraging female rape victims to marry their attackers. NGO Lawyers Collective noted the length of trials, lack of victim support, and inadequate protection of witnesses and victims remained major concerns. Doctors continued to carry out the invasive "two-finger test" to speculate sexual history, despite the Supreme Court holding that that the test violates a victim's right to privacy. In 2015 the government introduced new guidelines for health professionals for medical examinations of victims of sexual violence. It included provisions regarding consent of the victim during various stages of examination, which some NGOs claimed was an improvement to recording incidents. Some sources maintained that despite these directions, many medical professionals remained unaware of state guidelines for treating survivors of sexual violence.

Women in conflict areas, such as in Jammu and Kashmir, the northeast, Jharkhand, and Chhattisgarh, as well as vulnerable Dalit or tribal women, were often victims of rape or threats of rape. National crime statistics indicated Dalit women were disproportionately victimized compared with other caste affiliations.

The law provides for protection against some forms of abuse against women in the home, including verbal, emotional, and economic abuse, as well as the threat of abuse. The law recognizes the right of a woman to reside in a shared household with her spouse or partner while a dispute continues, although a woman may seek accommodations at the partner's expense. Although the law also provides women with the right to police assistance, legal aid, shelter, and medical care, domestic abuse remained a serious problem. Lack of law enforcement safeguards and pervasive corruption limited the effectiveness of the law.

The Ministry of Women and Child Development promulgated guidelines for the establishment of social services for women, but due to lack of funding, personnel, and proper training, services were primarily available only in metropolitan areas. Some police officials, especially in smaller towns, were reluctant to register cases of crimes against women, especially against persons of influence.

On May 17, the Ministry of Women and Child Development unveiled the "National Policy for Women 2016," a roadmap on women's issues for government action over the next 15 to 20 years. Drafted after consultations with NGOs and civil society, the policy addresses cybercrime, maternity leave, nutrition, education, and a review of the criminalization of marital rape among other issues.

Domestic violence continued to be a problem, and the National Family Health Survey revealed more than 50 percent of women reported experiencing some form of violence in their home. Advocates reported many women refrained from reporting domestic abuses due to social pressures. According to some NGOs, the lack of consolidated data was a disadvantage in framing policies and taking appropriate action. Attitudes of law enforcement officials treating domestic violence as a "private matter" also remained a concern for NGOs.

Gender-based violence remained one of the key issues facing women in Jammu and Kashmir. According to the state's Commission for Women, the number of incidents of crime against women registered an increase of about 11 percent in 2016 compared with 2015.

Crimes against women, including kidnapping, rape, dowry deaths, and domestic abuse, remained a significant problem. The NCRB noted underreporting of such crimes was likely. The NCRB estimated the conviction rate for crimes against women to be 19.6 percent. Acid attacks against women caused death and permanent disfigurement. According to the NCRB, the number of acid attack victims increased from 241 in 2014 to 305 in 2015, an increase of 27 percent.

Acid, commonly used as a household cleaner, was available at local markets. Despite a 2013 Supreme Court order regulating the sale of acid across the country, media reports indicated acid was easily available. In June 2015, pursuant to the Supreme Court directive, the Karnataka State Commission for Women increased compensation for acid and kerosene attack victims from 200,000 rupees ($3,000) to 300,000 rupees ($4,500). The sum awarded is irrespective of the degree of harm sustained. In April 2015 the Supreme Court directed all private hospitals to provide medical assistance to victims of acid attacks. During the year implementation of the policy began in Chennai.

In the first conviction for an acid attack in the country, on September 9, a special court convicted Ankur Panwar for a fatal acid attack of 23-year-old Preeti Rathi at a railway station in Mumbai in 2013. In July the central government launched a revised Central Victim Compensation Fund scheme to reduce disparities in compensation for victims of crime including rape, acid attacks, crime against children, and human trafficking across India. Started with a one-time grant of two billion rupees ($300 million) under the Nirbhaya Fund, the scheme will provide a minimum compensation of 300,000 rupees ($4,500) for acid attack victims. Compensation increases by 50 percent if the victim is less than 14.

Media reported rioters raped at least 10 women traveling on a national highway through Haryana on February 22. The alleged rapes occurred during a series of protests organized across Haryana, Uttar Pradesh, Rajasthan, and Delhi by the Jat community demanding reservations in government jobs. After initially denying the allegations, the Haryana government acknowledged to the Punjab and Haryana High Court in August that state police investigations indicated rapes appeared to have occurred. Although the report of the government-appointed Special Investigating Team was presented to the court, the government counsel claimed no witnesses came forward to file complaints. He also informed the court the investigation continued and that five persons had been arrested in connection to the case.

Female Genital Mutilation/Cutting (FGM/C): No national law addresses the practice of FGM/C. According to human rights groups and media reports, between 70 and 90 percent of Dawoodi Bohras, a population of approximately one million concentrated in Maharashtra and Gujarat, practiced various forms of FGM/C. On June 4, the Bohra spiritual head, Syedna Mufaddal Saifuddin, for the first time spoke publicly about the practice of FGM/C as an "act of religious purity," and a religious obligation for all women and girls in the community. Prior to this statement, local congregations had issued directives calling on their members to refrain from practicing FGM/C where the procedure is legally banned. On May 7, a rival claimant for the sect's leadership, Syedna Taher Fakhruddin, issued a public statement condemning FGM/C as "an un-Islamic and horrific practice" that should only be allowed after a girl attained adulthood and of her free volition.

Other Harmful Traditional Practices: The law forbids the provision or acceptance of a dowry, but families continued to offer and accept dowries, and dowry disputes remained a serious problem. The law also bans harassment in the form of dowry demands and empowers magistrates to issue protection orders. NCRB data showed authorities arrested 19,973 persons for dowry deaths in 2015.

"Sumangali schemes" affected an estimated 120,000 young women. These plans, named after the Tamil word for "happily married woman," are a form of bonded labor in which young women or girls work to earn money for a dowry to be able to marry. The promised lump-sum compensation ranged from 80,000 to 100,000 rupees ($1,200 to $1,500), which was withheld until the end of three to five years of employment. Compensation, however, sometimes went partially or entirely unpaid. While in bonded labor, employers reportedly subjected women to serious workplace abuses, severe restrictions on freedom of movement and communication, sexual abuse, sexual exploitation, sex trafficking, and murder. The majority of sumangali-bonded laborers came from the Scheduled Castes, and of those, employers subjected Dalits, the lowest-ranking Arunthathiyars, and migrants from northern India, to particular abuse. Authorities did not allow trade unions in sumangali factories, and some sumangali workers reportedly did not report abuses due to fear of retribution. A 2014 case study by NGO Vaan Muhil described health problems among workers and working conditions reportedly involving physical and sexual exploitation. In July the Madras High Court ordered the Tamil Nadu government to evaluate the legality of sumangali schemes.

Most states employed dowry prohibition officers, with the exception of Mizoram and Nagaland, states that do not have a tradition of dowry. The Dowry Prohibition Act does not apply to Jammu and Kashmir. A 2010 Supreme Court ruling makes it mandatory for all trial courts to charge defendants in dowry-death cases with murder.

So-called honor killings remained a problem, especially in Punjab, Uttar Pradesh, and Haryana. These states also had low female birth ratios due to gender-selective abortions. Some killings resulted from extrajudicial decisions by traditional community elders, such as "khap panchayats," unelected caste-based village assemblies that have no legal standing. The NGO Center for Social Research conducted extensive awareness campaigns in several districts in Haryana and noted that khap panchayats had not publicly deliberated on the issue of honor killings during the year. In December Junior Home Minister Hansraj Ahir told lawmakers that police registered 251 cases of honor killing in 2015, compared with 28 in 2014 when the country began counting them separately from murder. The most common justification for the killings cited by the accused or by their relatives was that the victim married against her family's wishes. Statistics for honor killings remained difficult to verify since many killings were either unreported or reported as natural deaths or suicides by family members.

There were reports women and girls in the "devadasi" system of symbolic marriages to Hindu deities were victims of rape or sexual abuse at the hands of priests and temple patrons--a form of sex trafficking. NGOs suggested families forced some SC girls into prostitution in temples to mitigate household financial burdens and the prospect of marriage dowries. Some states have laws to curb prostitution or sexual abuse of women and girls in temple service. Enforcement of these laws remained lax, and the problem was widespread. Some observers estimated more than 450,000 women and girls engaged in temple-related prostitution.

There was no federal law addressing accusations of witchcraft; however, authorities can use provisions under the penal code as an alternative for a victim accused of witchcraft. Bihar, Odisha, Chhattisgarh, Rajasthan, Assam, and Jharkhand have laws criminalizing those who accuse others of witchcraft. In August 2015 the Assam state legislature unanimously passed a law making "witch-hunting" a criminal offense. Most reports stated villagers and local council usually banned the accused from the village. The Committee for Skeptical Inquiry think tank reported many accusations and related violence have roots in property disputes and local politics.

According to a Partners for Law in Development on Contemporary Practices of Witch Hunting 2015 study, special laws against witch hunting were rarely, if at all, invoked in Chhattisgarh, Bihar, and Jharkhand, where the fieldwork for the study was undertaken. The study claimed action was more likely under the penal code when violence escalated and preventive action was unlikely.

More than a year after Rajasthan passed its 2015 Prevention of Witch Hunting Bill, victims were still awaiting justice. While official figures showed approximately 20 women were accused of witchcraft in Bhilwara, NGOs stated there were 61 cases of witch hunting between 1998 and 2016. Women were killed in three cases, and the accused were in jail briefly before they were granted bail. The NHRC issued a notice to the Rajasthan government regarding the plight of women accused of witchcraft in Rajasthan's Bhilwara District.

Discrimination against widows occurred throughout the country. According to some cultural traditions, widows were inauspicious and sometimes cast out by their own families. Many widows became destitute and resorted to begging for survival.

Sexual Harassment: Authorities required all state departments and institutions with more than 50 employees to operate committees to prevent and address sexual harassment, often referred to as "Eve teasing." By law sexual harassment includes one or more unwelcome acts or behavior, such as physical contact, a request for sexual favors, making sexually suggestive remarks, or showing pornography. Employers who fail to establish complaint committees faced fines of up to 50,000 rupees ($750). The law also includes penalties for false or malicious charges.

Reproductive Rights: Lack of access to quality reproductive and maternal health care services, skilled attendants at birth, contraception to space pregnancies, and unsafe abortion continued to contribute to high rates of maternal mortality. According to UN estimates, the maternal mortality ratio was 174 deaths per 100,000 live births in 2015. A woman's lifetime risk of maternal death was one in 220, and 45,000 women died during pregnancy and childbirth. The 2010-12 Sample Registration Report of the registrar general, released in 2013, showed during three years Assam's maternal mortality rate was the highest in the country at 300, followed by Uttar Pradesh/Uttarakhand at 285. Kerala at 66, Maharashtra at 68, and Tamil Nadu at 79 had the lowest rates. Maternal mortality rates were difficult to calculate in many northeast states, which suffered from inadequate infrastructure and insufficiently trained medical staff.

According to the law, contraceptive information and services must be available, accessible, acceptable, and of reliable quality. Official policy promotes the right of a woman to access contraceptive information and services; however, there were often limited resources available. UN research in 2015 indicated 13 percent of married women between the ages of 15 and 49 did not wish to have additional children or wished to space births but could not access contraception.

Some women reportedly were pressured to have tubal ligations, hysterectomies, or other forms of sterilization because of the payment structures for health workers and insurance payments for private facilities. This pressure appeared to affect disproportionately poor and lower-caste women. In September the Supreme Court ordered the closure of all sterilization camps within three years, citing concerns regarding unsafe and unsanitary conditions that resulted in high rates of illness and mortality.

Although the government achieved a significant increase in institutional births, there were reports health facilities continued to be overburdened, underequipped, and undersupplied, in addition to demonstrating substandard regard for hygiene and patient dignity.

In community health centers, 70 percent of gynecologist positions remained unfilled, according to a 2012 report by the Ministry of Health and Family Welfare on rural health statistics. Only 13 percent of the centers had the requisite number of specialists. Poor health infrastructure disproportionately affected marginalized women, including homeless, Dalit and tribal women, those working on tea estates or in the informal labor sector, and women with disabilities.

The government permitted health clinics and local NGOs to operate freely in disseminating information about family planning. The country continued nevertheless to have unmet needs for contraception, deaths related to unsafe abortion, maternal mortality, and coercive family planning practices, including coerced or unethical sterilization and policies restricting access to entitlements for women with more than two children. Policies and guideline initiatives penalizing families with more than two children remained in place in seven states, but some authorities did not enforce them. Certain states maintained government reservations for government jobs and subsidies for adults with no more than two children and reduced subsidies and access to health care for those who have more than two.

Rajasthan, one of 11 states to adopt a two-child limit for elected officials at the local level, was the first to adopt the law in 1992. Despite efforts at the state level to reverse or amend the law, it remained unchanged during the year. Originally seen as a targeted way to reduce family size, a 2015 study by Ideas for India indicated the law resulted in reduced birthrates but had a negative impact on the male to female sex ratio.

Government efforts to reduce the fertility rate were occasionally coercive during the year. Authorities in some areas paid health workers and facilities in some areas a fixed amount for each sterilization procedure and reviewed them against quotas for female sterilizations. In some states authorities threatened health workers with pay cuts or dismissal for failing to meet quotas. Some reports described a "sterilization season," in which health-care workers pressed to reach quotas for sterilizations before the end of the fiscal year on March 31. Some doctors reportedly withheld health services unless a woman agreed to sterilization.

Women reportedly were more likely to be sterilized after they had given birth to at least one son.

Although national health officials noted the central government did not have the authority to regulate state decisions on population issues, the central government creates guidelines and funds state level reproductive health programs. A 2005 Supreme Court decision deemed the national government responsible for providing quality care for sterilization services at the state level. Almost all states also introduced "girl child promotion" schemes, intended to counter sex selection, some of which required a certificate of sterilization for the parents to collect benefits. Administrative hurdles and high demands for documentation reportedly made these schemes inaccessible to many marginalized families.

According to a 2013 National Health Survey, health workers had sterilized more than one in three women between the ages of 15 and 45. One in two women over the age of 35 was sterilized. Most sterilizations were performed on women when they were between the ages of 20 and 35, but one out of every hundred teenage girls was also sterilized. According to the same survey, on average three women died every week from botched sterilizations. The government has aggressively promoted female sterilization as a form of family planning for decades and, as a result, female sterilization comprised 63 percent of all contraceptive use in the country. The HRLN filed more than a dozen complaints regarding the government's failure to provide counseling and information on the Family

Planning Indemnity Scheme on behalf of women who received failed sterilizations or died in the government health camps.

There were no formal restrictions on the right to access contraceptives, but the government sometimes promoted permanent female sterilization to the exclusion of alternate forms of contraception. Repeated studies by the government and NGOs suggested most women had little familiarity with nonpermanent forms of contraceptives offered through the public health system, such as birth control pills, intrauterine devices, and condoms. The highest unmet need for contraceptives reportedly was among women with one child who wanted to delay a second pregnancy. Reports from NGOs claimed pharmacists across the country, especially in Maharashtra, limited women's access to legal over-the-counter emergency contraceptive pills and to legal medical termination prescription drugs.

<u>Discrimination</u>: The law prohibits discrimination in the workplace and requires equal pay for equal work, but employers sometimes paid women less than men for the same job, discriminated against women in employment and credit applications, and promoted women less frequently than men.

Many tribal land systems, including in Bihar, deny tribal women the right to own land. Muslim personal law traditionally governs land inheritance for Muslim women, allotting them less than allotted to men. Other laws relating to the ownership of assets and land accord women little control over land use, retention, or sale. Several exceptions existed, such as in Kerala, Ladakh District, Meghalaya, and Himachal Pradesh, where women control family property and have inheritance rights.

In January the Bihar government approved a 35 percent quota for women in state government jobs at all levels.

<u>Gender-biased Sex Selection</u>: According to the latest census (2011), the national average male-female sex ratio at birth was 1,000 to 943. In 2011 the national child sex ratio, covering children between ages zero and six, was 1,000 boys to 918 girls. The state of Kerala had the lowest male-female sex ratio at birth at 1,000 to 1,084, and the state of Haryana had the highest ratio, at 1,000 to 877. A 2002 law prohibits prenatal sex selection, but authorities rarely enforced it. When state governments obtained convictions, doctors did not always lose their professional license, although the Medical Council in 2015 canceled the license to practice medicine of six doctors from Maharashtra convicted under the law.

In October 2015 the Delhi government issued "show-cause" notices to 89 hospitals and diagnostic centers with sex ratios at birth significantly lower than the state average. The average sex ratio in Delhi is 896 females for every 1,000 males. Based on the results of a survey conducted by the Delhi Health Ministry, these 89 institutions exposed sex ratios ranged from 285 to 788 live female births for every 1,000 male births.

Numerous NGOs throughout the country and some states attempted to increase awareness of the problem of prenatal sex selection, promote female births, and prevent female infanticide and abandonment.

Children

Birth Registration: The law establishes state government procedures for birth registration. The UN Children's Fund (UNICEF) estimated authorities registered 58 percent of national births each year. Children lacking citizenship or registration may not be able to access public services, enroll in school, or obtain identification documents later in life.

Education: The constitution provides for free education for all children from ages six to 14, but the government did not always comply with this requirement. The NGO Pratham's 2013 *Annual Survey of Education* claimed only 70 percent of girls enrolled in primary school actually attended classes in 2013. The same report noted in the states of Uttar Pradesh, Bihar, Manipur, West Bengal, Jharkhand, and Madhya Pradesh, attendance was less than 60 percent. Girls between ages 11 and 14 were most frequently not enrolled.

There were numerous reports of schools refusing admission to underprivileged students.

Child Abuse: The law prohibits child abuse, but it does not recognize physical abuse by caregivers, neglect, or psychological abuse as punishable offenses. All types of abuse remained common, including in school and institutional settings. The government often failed to educate the public adequately against child abuse or to enforce the law. Although banned, teachers often used corporal punishment.

According to the NGO Global Perspectives' August 2015 report, the number of abused children in the country was 200,000. In a 2014 study published by the *Journal of Anxiety Disorders* on 702 adolescents from Jammu and Kashmir between the ages of 13 to 17 years, boys reported a higher rate of sexual abuse than dido girls (57 percent compared with 35 percent).

The government sponsored a toll-free 24-hour helpline for children in distress working with 640 partners in 402 locations. A network of NGOs staffed the "Childline 1098 Service" number, accessible by either a child or an adult to request immediate assistance, including medical care, shelter, restoration, rescue, sponsorship, and counseling.

On August 26, the Ministry of Women and Child Development launched an "e-box" for online and confidential registration of child sexual abuse complaints. The Minister of Women and Child Development Maneka Gandhi stated victims generally do not report offenses since the offenders are often family members, relatives, or acquaintances. The e-box is hosted on the home page of the National Commission for Protection of Child Rights.

Early and Forced Marriage: The law sets the legal age of marriage for women at 18 and men at 21, and it empowers courts to annul child marriages. It also sets penalties for persons who perform, arrange, or participate in such marriages. NGOs assess that reporting of early and forced marriage remains low. Authorities did not consistently enforce the law nor address rape of girls forced into marriage. Some religiously based personal laws allow marriages at an age earlier than the general law. The law does not characterize a marriage between a girl below age 18 and a boy below age 21 as "illegal," but it recognizes such unions as voidable, providing grounds for challenging them in court. Only the party who was a minor at the time of marriage may seek nullification. If the party is still a minor, his or her guardian must file a petition for nullification. A party may also file upon becoming an adult but must do so within two years. According to international and local NGOs, these limitations effectively left married minors with no legal remedy in most situations.

The law establishes a full-time child-marriage prohibition officer in every state to prevent and police child marriage. These individuals have the power to intervene when a child marriage is taking place, document violations of the law, file charges against parents, remove children from dangerous situations, and deliver them to local child-protection authorities.

UNICEF's *State of the World's Children 2016* report noted between 2008 and 2014, 47 percent of girls married before age 18, and 18 percent were married before the age of 15. According to the report, women married as children contributed to the country's high infant and maternal mortality rates, and observers estimated early motherhood contributed to the deaths of 6,000 adolescent mothers each year. The most recent National Family Health Survey, conducted in 2005-2006, showed one in six girls between the ages of 15 and 19 had become pregnant at least once.

Female Genital Mutilation/Cutting (FGM/C): See information in the women's section above.

Sexual Exploitation of Children: The law prohibits child pornography and sets the legal age of consent at 18. It is illegal to pay for sex with a minor, to induce a minor into prostitution or any form of "illicit sexual intercourse," or to sell or buy a minor for the purposes of prostitution. Violators are subject to 10 years' imprisonment and a fine.

NGOs reported children under age 18 forced into prostitution in red-light districts in major cities. Child trafficking for sexual exploitation frequently occurred in urban and rural areas. The Ministry of Home Affairs stated criminals subjected significant numbers of missing children to trafficking after the children ran away from home.

Special Courts to try child sexual abuse cases under the Protection of Children from Sexual Offenses Act, 2012 existed in all six Delhi courts. Civil society groups observed, however, that large caseloads severely limited judges' abilities to take on cases in a timely manner. Hearings were regularly adjourned with long delays between hearing dates, sometimes as long as nine months.

In March NGO Gopabandhu Seva Parishad, which worked in an urban slum in Puri, Odisha, stated that child sex tourism continued to flourish in tourist areas. They claimed boys between eight and 13 years of age were more vulnerable to sexual abuse than girls. The NGO recorded 106 cases of abuse during their interaction with the local community between 2013 and 2015.

On November 5, the Maharashtra state government shut down a government-run residential school for tribal children in Buldhana District after media reported at least two girls were raped at the school. The government suspended the school's entire teaching and administrative staff, and police arrested 15 persons including school officials, teachers, and a former village council chief.

<u>Child Soldiers</u>: No information was available on how many persons under age 18 were serving in the armed forces. NGO estimated there were at least 2,500 children associated with insurgent armed groups in Maoist-affected areas. There were allegations government-supported, anti-Maoist village defense forces recruited children. Armed insurgent groups, including Maoists in the northeast states and Islamist groups in Jammu and Kashmir reportedly used children (see section 1.g.).

<u>Displaced Children</u>: Displaced children, including refugees, IDPs, and street children, faced restrictions on access to government services (see also section 2.d.) and were often unable to obtain medical care, education, proper nutrition, or shelter. Employers often abused such children physically and sexually and forced them to work in hazardous jobs, such as rag picking (sorting garbage for recyclables).

<u>Institutionalized Children</u>: Lax law enforcement and a lack of safeguards encouraged an atmosphere of impunity in a number of group homes and orphanages. NGOs alleged many such homes for children operated without government oversight or approval. Only 14 states had commissions for the protection of child rights, as mandated by law. On April 15, video footage from closed circuit cameras installed in a government-run childcare center in Karimnagar, Telangana, showed two women caretakers branding three children with a hot spoon as punishment for not eating food. District authorities suspended three caretakers, and police later arrested the two main accused. The children were relocated to another home for medical treatment and care.

The Calcutta Research Group reported police separated families detained at the India-Bangladesh border in the state of West Bengal by institutionalizing children in Juvenile Justice Homes with limited and restricted access to their families.

<u>International Child Abductions</u>: The country is not a party to the 1980 Hague Convention on the Civil Aspects of International Child Abduction. See the Department of State's *Annual Report on International Parental Child Abduction* at travel.state.gov/content/childabduction/en/legal/compliance.html.

Anti-Semitism

Jewish groups from the 4,650-member Jewish community cited no reports of anti-Semitic acts during the year. In May Minister of State for Minority Affairs Mukhtar Abbas Naqvi told members of parliament the central government did not have a timeline for declaring Jews as a minority community. In June Maharashtra became the second state in the country to grant minority status to the Jewish community, which ensures Jews are separately counted by the census.

Trafficking in Persons

See the Department of State's *Trafficking in Persons Report* at www.state.gov/j/tip/rls/tiprpt/.

Persons with Disabilities

The constitution does not explicitly mention disability as a prohibited ground for discrimination. The Persons with Disabilities Act provides equal rights for persons with a variety of disabilities, including blindness, hearing disability, Hansen's disease (leprosy), mobility disability, developmental disability, and mental disability. The law links implementation of programs to the "economic capacity and development" of the government. The act encourages governmental authorities to promote access, but it includes no specific enforcement provisions or sanctions for noncompliance.

According to the director of the National Center for Promotion of Employment for Disabled People, the law regards persons with disabilities as requiring social protection and medical care, rather than as possessing inherent rights as persons with disabilities.

Discrimination against persons with disabilities in employment, education, and access to health care was more pervasive in rural areas. The Kolkata High Court passed an order in 2013 mandating the state government to provide accessibility to roads and buildings. Despite legislation that all public buildings and transport be accessible to persons with disabilities, there was limited accessibility. A Public Interest File was pending in the Supreme Court on accessibility to buildings and roads.

A Department of School Education and Literacy program provided special educators and resource centers for students with disabilities. There was no data available on whether these students remained within the education system or if the system denied any individualized supports needed for their education. The law allows mainstream schools to admit children with disabilities, but mainstream schools remained inadequately equipped with teachers trained in inclusive education, resource material, and appropriate curricula.

In April, 11 residents with disabilities, including at least seven children, died at a government-run rehabilitation institute near Jaipur, Rajasthan, allegedly after drinking contaminated water. The NHRC issued notices to the Rajasthan government for failure to maintain the facility.

The law also reserves 3 percent of all educational places for persons with disabilities, although students with disabilities comprised only an estimated 1 percent of all students, according to the Ministry of Social Justice and Empowerment.

Some schools continued to segregate children with disabilities or deny them enrollment due to lack of infrastructure, equipment, and trained staff. The Ministry of Social Justice and Empowerment continued to offer scholarships to persons with disabilities to pursue higher education. University enrollment of students with disabilities remained low for several reasons, including inaccessible infrastructure, limited resources, nonimplementation of the 3 percent job reservation, and harassment.

The Ministry of Health and Family Welfare estimated 6 to 7 percent of the population experienced a mental or psychosocial disability. Of the individuals with mental disabilities, 25 percent were homeless, and many in rural areas did not have access to modern mental health-care facilities. Disability rights activists estimated there were 40 to 90 million persons with disabilities. There were three mental-health institutions run by the federal government and 40 state-operated mental hospitals. According to the Department of Empowerment of Persons with Disabilities' 2016 annual report and 2011 Census data, 49.5 percent of persons with disabilities were issued disability certificates until August 2015.

Patients in some mental-health institutions faced food shortages, inadequate sanitary conditions, and lack of adequate medical care. Human Rights Watch reported women and girls with disabilities occasionally were forced into mental hospitals against their will.

On August 18, the NHRC issued notice to the government of West Bengal over alleged hazardous conditions of 430 residents at the Berhampore Mental Hospital. The commission took into account an NGO's report that men and women with mental disabilities had not bathed or shaved for months and were lying without clothing on unsanitary floors. The NHRC sought a status report on all mental hospitals run by the state from the special rapporteur and chief secretary.

Most persons with mental disabilities depended on public health-care facilities, and fewer than half who required treatment or community support services received such assistance.

Persons with disabilities reported cases of discrimination by the Central Industrial Security Forces in airports despite framed guidelines providing for no discrimination based on disability in air travel.

The law reserves 3 percent of public-sector jobs for persons with physical, hearing, or vision disabilities. On June 30, the Supreme Court decided the implementation of policies granting rights to persons with disabilities remained inadequate and overruled the central government's prior orders restricting reservation of jobs for persons with disabilities to the higher echelons of government service. The court directed the government to extend the 3 percent reservation to all government posts. In August Personnel, Public Grievances, and Pensions Minister of State Jitendra Singh informed members of parliament that a special government recruitment drive for persons with disabilities was launched in May 2015, resulting in the recruitment of 12,377 positions for 15,831 identified vacancies. Data on representation of persons with disabilities in different departments and ministries indicated an increase from 7,368 employees across 78 departments of the central government in January 2012 to 20,520 employees in 58 departments and ministries in January 2015.

The government continued to allocate funds to programs and NGO partners to increase the number of jobs filled. Private-sector employment of persons with disabilities remained low, despite governmental incentives that private companies establish a workforce of more than 5 percent with persons with disabilities.

In February advocacy groups organized a protest in Chennai against the inclusion of the term "destitute" in Tamil Nadu's "Destitute Differently Abled Pension Scheme" and demanded less stringent conditions for pension eligibility. According to civil society, hundreds of protesters, including many with physical disabilities, were taken into custody on February 17 and held in a stadium that lacked accessible facilities. Police released the protesters, but hundreds chose to remain. On February 22, the Tamil Nadu Social Welfare and Nutritious Meal Program Department changed the eligibility criteria and removed "destitute" from the act's name.

National/Racial/Ethnic Minorities

The national census categorized the population by language spoken, not by racial or ethnic groups. Traditionally, large segments of society are organized into castes or clans. Caste is a complex social hierarchy system that traditionally determines ritual purity and occupation. The constitution in 1949 prohibits caste discrimination. The registration of castes and tribes continued for the purpose of affirmative action programs, as the government implemented programs to empower members of the low castes. The law gives the president authority to identify disadvantaged castes and tribes for special quotas and benefits. Discrimination based on caste remained prevalent particularly in rural areas. According to a 2014 survey by the Indian National Council of Applied Economic Research and the University of Maryland, 27 percent of Indian households practice caste-based untouchability, with the highest untouchability practices found in Madhya Pradesh, Chhattisgarh, Rajasthan, Bihar, and Uttar Pradesh.

The term "Dalit," derived from the Sanskrit for "oppressed" or "crushed," refers to members of what society regarded as the lowest Hindu castes, the Scheduled Castes (SC). Many SC members continued to face impediments to the means of social advancement, including education, jobs, access to justice, freedom of movement, and access to institutions and services. According to the 2011 census, SC members constituted 17 percent (approximately 200 million persons) of the population.

Although the law protects Dalits, there were numerous reports of violence and significant discrimination in access to services, such as health care, education, temple attendance, and marriage. Many Dalits were malnourished. Most bonded laborers were Dalits. Dalits who asserted their rights were often victims of attacks, especially in rural areas. As agricultural laborers for higher-caste landowners, Dalits reportedly often worked without monetary remuneration. Reports from the UN Committee on the Elimination of Racial Discrimination described systematic abuse of Dalits, including extrajudicial killings and sexual violence against Dalit women. Crimes committed against Dalits reportedly often went unpunished, either because authorities failed to prosecute perpetrators or because victims did not report crimes due to fear of retaliation.

NGOs reported widespread discrimination, including prohibiting Dalits from walking on public pathways, wearing footwear, accessing water from public taps in upper-caste neighborhoods, participating in some temple festivals, bathing in public pools, or using certain cremation grounds. In Gujarat, for example, Dalits were reportedly denied entry to temples and denied educational and employment opportunities. In Odisha, on June 3, a mob of upper-caste individuals allegedly burned 11 Dalit homes. A human rights NGO stated in a report that the arson occurred due to a dispute in February over the alleged caricaturing of Dalits by upper-caste villagers in a play. The NGO alleged the Dalit families faced a boycott and were denied access to shops and sources of potable water. Police lodged an FIR against 19 persons under the Scheduled Castes and Scheduled Tribes (Prevention of Atrocities) Act, but no arrests were made.

NGOs reported that Dalit students were sometimes denied admission to certain schools because of their caste or were required to present caste certification prior to admission. There were reports that school officials barred Dalit children from morning prayers, asked Dalit children to sit in the back of the class, or forced them to clean school toilets while denying them access to the same facilities. There were also reports that teachers refused to correct the homework of Dalit children, refused to provide midday meals to Dalit children, and asked Dalit children to sit separately from children of upper-caste families. In April Social Justice and Empowerment Minister of State Vijay Sampla told members of parliament the government did not have data regarding atrocities against Dalits in educational institutions.

On January 17, a University of Hyderabad doctoral Dalit student Rohith Vemula committed suicide after he and four others were suspended for allegedly beating another student. Vemula's suicide sparked nationwide protests by students and activists calling for reforms in higher education to bar caste-based discrimination. The Human Resource Development ministry constituted a fact-finding committee, which acknowledged "the feeling of deprivation and discrimination among students from the socially and economically weaker sections" on the campus.

The federal and state governments continued to implement programs for SC members to provide better-quality housing, reserved seats in schools, government jobs, and access to subsidized foods, but critics claimed many of these programs suffered from poor implementation and/or corruption.

Manual scavenging--the removal of animal or human waste by Dalits--continued in spite of its legal prohibition. NGO activists claimed elected village councils employed a majority of manual scavengers that belonged to Other Backward Classes and Dalit populations. Media regularly published articles and pictures of persons cleaning manholes and sewers without protective gear. According to a March report from the UN special rapporteur on minority issues, local governments and municipalities continue to employ manual scavengers despite a legislative prohibition. Officials countered the special rapporteur had exceeded her mandate, which was to promote the human rights of persons belonging to "national, or ethnic, religious minorities," and therefore inapplicable to caste groups.

Human Rights Watch reported that children of manual scavengers faced discrimination, humiliation, and segregation at village schools. Their occupation often exposed manual scavengers to infections that affected their skin, eyes, respiratory, and gastrointestinal systems. Health practitioners suggested children exposed to such bacteria were often unable to maintain a healthy body weight and suffered from stunted growth.

The law prohibits the employment of scavengers or the construction of dry (nonflush) latrines, and penalties range from imprisonment for up to one year, a fine of 2,000 rupees ($30), or both. Nonetheless, Indian Railways acknowledged that it fitted approximately 30,000 passenger coaches with open-discharge toilets, "forcing" the railways to employ manual scavengers to clean the tracks. The railways proposed to install sealed toilet systems but without a fixed timeline for implementation.

In March media reported hundreds of Dalit bonded laborers protested caste discrimination outside the Uttarakhand Assembly and State Human Rights Commission. The protesters had reportedly fled their homes after decades of alleged oppression. The protesters petitioned the commission to take punitive action against state revenue police for alleged harassment and failure to register their complaints.

There were more than 50,000 Indian citizens of African descent, or "Siddis," mostly descendants of Bantu people from East Africa brought to India as slaves from the eighth to nineteenth centuries. Residing primarily in Karnataka, Maharashtra, Andhra Pradesh, West Bengal, and Gujarat, Siddis were classified as "Scheduled Tribes" in 2003, but remained one of the poorest, most isolated, and economically disadvantaged groups in the country according to NGOs, which observe that Siddis continued to face widespread racial discrimination outside their communities.

Incidents of attacks against African nationals were reported during the year. On January 31, a Sudanese national allegedly drove his car over a 35-year-old Indian woman, killing her. A neighborhood mob set the car on fire as the suspect fled. The mob then pulled a Tanzanian woman from her car as she and two other students drove by the scene. She was chased, stripped, and sexually assaulted. The Tanzanian High Commission registered a complaint prompting External Affairs Minister Sushma Swaraj and Karnataka Chief Minister K. Siddaramaiah to launch an investigation. The Ministries of External Affairs and of Home Affairs launched racism sensitization programs in neighborhoods focused on neighborhoods where people of African origin reside.

Indigenous People

The constitution provides for the social, economic, and political rights of disadvantaged groups of indigenous people. The law provides special status for indigenous people, but authorities often denied them their rights. There were more than 700 Scheduled Tribes (STs) in the country, and the 2011 census revealed the population of ST members as 84.3 million, approximately 8 percent of the total population. In 2011 a pilot survey to identify households below the poverty line found that ST and SC members constituted half the total of poor households. There were 75 particularly vulnerable tribal groups, characterized by primitive technology, stagnant or declining population, extremely low literacy, and a subsistence-level economy.

In most of the northeastern states, where indigenous groups constituted the majority of the states' populations, laws provide for tribal rights, although some local authorities disregarded these provisions. The laws prohibit any nontribal person, including citizens from other states, from crossing a government-established inner boundary without a valid permit. No one can remove rubber, wax, ivory, or other forest products from protected areas without authorization. Tribal authorities must approve the sale of land to nontribal persons.

There were reports that tribal women employed as domestic workers often were neither properly paid nor protected from sexual exploitation. Encroachment on tribal lands continued in almost every state, despite efforts to combat the practice, since businesses and private parties continued to exert political pressure against local governments. Those displaced by the encroachments typically did not receive appropriate compensation.

Tribal movements demanded the protection of tribal land and property. Local activists claimed that authorities continued to ignore the rights of tribal and rural groups under the Forest Act. Weak enforcement of the act often circumvented the free and informed consent of tribal and rural groups prior to development.

Local villagers, many of whom are members of STs and oppose iron ore mining in insurgency-hit Kanker District in southern Chattisgarh, said there was an increased presence of paramilitary personnel from the Border Security Force. Villagers who protested the use of forest land for mining complained of arbitrary detentions, arrests, and false charges of linkages with Maoist (Naxalite) insurgents.

Acts of Violence, Discrimination, and Other Abuses Based on Sexual Orientation and Gender Identity

The law criminalizes homosexual sex. Lesbian, gay, bisexual, transgender, and intersex (LGBTI) persons faced physical attacks, rape, and blackmail. Some police committed crimes against LGBTI persons and used the threat of arrest to coerce victims not to report the incidents. Several states, with the aid of NGOs, offered education and sensitivity training to police.

LGBTI groups reported they faced widespread societal discrimination and violence, particularly in rural areas. Activists reported that transgender persons, who were HIV positive, continued to face difficulty obtaining medical treatment. Advocacy organizations, such as the Mission for Indian Gay and Lesbian Empowerment, documented workplace discrimination against LGBTI persons, including slurs and unjustified dismissals. In June NGO MINGLE released results of its survey of LGBTI employees from the information technology, banking, and manufacturing sectors on workplace climate, which showed that 40 percent of LGBTI persons faced some form of harassment.

In January 2015 a high court dismissed petitions challenging the 2013 Supreme Court judgment reinstating a colonial-era penal code provision criminalizing homosexual sex. The Supreme Court ruled that only parliament may change Section 377 of the Indian Penal Code, the law that bans consensual same-sex sexual activity. Media, activists, prominent individuals, and some government officials strongly criticized the ruling. In June the Supreme Court refused to hear a petition challenging Section 377, and petitioners were asked to apply to the chief justice of India, who was hearing a separate case to strike down the ban.

In March 2015 Tamil Nadu Uniformed Services Recruitment Board rejected K. Prathika Yashini's application because her name did not match her birth name, "K. Pradeep Kumar." Yashini previously changed her name with all government agencies after undergoing gender reassignment surgery. Yashini successfully sued in Madras High Court for permission to take a written examination for the police force. Yashini received appointment orders in February. Media reported that Tamil Nadu police offered positions to 21 other transgender persons.

HIV and AIDS Social Stigma

The number of new HIV cases decreased by 57 percent over the past decade. Of the estimated 2.09 million citizens infected with HIV, 39 percent were women and 7 percent were children under 15 years. Despite significant progress over the past 10 years, the epidemic persisted among the most vulnerable populations: high-risk groups, which include female sex workers; men who have sex with men; transgender persons; and persons who inject drugs.

The country has punitive laws criminalizing sex work. While the government focused on high-risk groups, civil society organizations committed to HIV work raised concern when the Supreme Court failed to overturn a section of the penal code that criminalizes same-gender sex acts. Additionally, antiretroviral drug stock outages in a few states led to treatment interruption.

The National AIDS Control Program prioritized HIV prevention, care, and treatment interventions for high-risk groups and rights of People Living with HIV. The program addressed stigma and discrimination by training health workers; mainstreaming the HIV response across the government; and promoting campaigns in health, work, and community settings to inform people with HIV/AIDS and high-risk groups of their rights and available services and to engage them in planning, monitoring, and evaluating HIV programs.

HIV/AIDS infection rates for women were highest in urban communities, while care was reportedly least available in rural areas. Early marriage, limited access to information and education, and limited access to health services, continued to leave women especially vulnerable to infection. The National AIDS Control Organization worked actively with NGOs to train women's HIV/AIDS self-help groups.

Police engaged in programs to strengthen their role in protecting communities vulnerable to human rights violations and HIV. Similarly, social protection initiatives integrated with an AIDS response showed risk reduction and improved health-seeking behavior, including uptake of and adherence to HIV treatment.

On June 24, a child rights activist complained to district officials in Kendrapara, Odisha that a central government-run residential school did not allow a 13-year-old girl suffering from HIV/AIDS to stay in the school hostel after objections from the parents of other students. The activist contended that although the school eventually permitted her to continue with her education, the principal's action violated the student's right to privacy and dignity.

Other Societal Violence or Discrimination

Societal violence based on religion and caste and by religiously associated groups continued to be a concern.

According to media reports, on July 11, seven Dalit men were reportedly stripped and publicly beaten by a Hindu mob for skinning dead cows. Police arrested 35 persons for the attack and suspended four police officers for negligence. Similarly, on July 26, a video uploaded by an eyewitness purportedly showed cow protection vigilantes beating two Muslim women outside a railway station in Mandsaur, Madhya Pradesh, as police watched from a distance. The police reportedly later arrested the women for beef possession. Although the meat was later determined to be buffalo, a local court charged the women with unlawful possession of meat and released them on bail on June 27. Police later arrested the two men accused of assaulting the women.

Ministry of Home Affairs data showed 751 incidents of communal violence took place, which killed 97 persons and injured 2,264.

On July 30, members of a right-wing Hindu group were charged with trespassing at the St. Thomas Aided Higher Primary School near Mangaluru and disrupting an Arabic class. The individuals reportedly accused the teacher of spreading extremism and seized textbooks from the children. The school suspended Urdu and Arabic classes after threats of further protests.

On June 28, Madurai-based NGO Evidence reported that some police personnel harassed and threatened its staff after the organization agreed to support the marriage of an inter-caste couple.

Civil society activists continued to express concern concerning the Gujarat government's failure to hold accountable those responsible for the 2002 communal violence in Gujarat that resulted in the deaths of more than 1,200 persons, the majority of whom were Muslim.

On July 27, the Gujarat High court sentenced seven individuals to life imprisonment for killing three Muslims near a railway crossing in Viramgam, during the 2002 Gujarat communal violence. Life terms were also upheld for two persons previously convicted. The trial court previously found four guilty of lesser offenses and acquitted three of the accused.

On August 4, the Gujarat High Court sentenced to life imprisonment 11 of the 27 accused of burning a father and his daughter to death in Mehsana in 2002, during the communal riots. The Mehsana Fast Track Court had previously acquitted all 27 accused in 2005. The defense lawyer for the convicted stated that four of the 11 were still missing when the court ordered them to surrender within 10 weeks.

Section 7. Worker Rights

a. Freedom of Association and the Right to Collective Bargaining

The law provides for the right to form and join unions and bargain collectively, although there is no legal obligation for employers to recognize a union or engage in collective bargaining. In the state of Sikkim, trade union registration was subject to prior permission from the state government. The law limits the organizing rights of federal and state government employees.

The law provides for the right to strike but places restrictions on this right for some workers. For instance, in export processing zones (EPZs), a 45-day notice is required because of the EPZs' designations as "public utilities." The law also allows the government to ban strikes in government-owned enterprises and requires arbitration in specified "essential industries." Definitions of essential industries vary from state to state. The law prohibits antiunion discrimination and retribution for involvement in legal strikes and provides for reinstatement of employees fired for union activity.

Enforcement of the law varied from state to state and from sector to sector. Enforcement was generally better in the larger, organized-sector industries. Authorities generally prosecuted and punished individuals responsible for intimidation or suppression of legitimate trade union activities in the industrial sector. Civil judicial procedures addressed violations because the Trade Union Act does not specify penalties for such violations. Specialized labor courts adjudicate labor disputes, but there were long delays and a backlog of unresolved cases.

Employers generally respected freedom of association and the right to organize and bargain collectively in the formal industrial sector but not in the large, informal economy. Most union members worked in the formal sector, and trade unions represented a small number of agricultural and informal-sector workers. An estimated 80 percent of unionized workers affiliated with one of the five major trade union federations. Unions were independent of the government, but four of the five major federations were associated with major political parties. According to the Ministry of Labor and Employment, there were 121 strikes and lockouts in 2014. State and local authorities occasionally used their power to declare strikes illegal and force adjudication. Membership-based organizations, such as the Self Employed Women's Association, successfully organized informal-sector workers and helped them to gain higher payment for their work or products.

On March 22, police detained the president of the Maruti Suzuki Workers Union in Gurgaon, Haryana, for leading a February 19 protest following an attack on a Honda Motorcycle and Scooters India employee by his supervisor, allegedly for refusing to work overtime. The union president was released from police custody in April.

On September 2, Haryana police detained 12 workers of Maruti Suzuki for distributing leaflets that urged workers to join the September 5 national strike. Labor groups reported that some employers continued to refuse to recognize established unions, and they established "workers' committees" and employer-controlled unions to prevent independent unions from being established. EPZs often employed workers on temporary contracts. Additionally, employee-only restrictions on entry to the EPZs limited union organizers' access.

On June 2, Karnataka police arrested Karnataka Police Association president Shashidhar Venugopal and Working Police Families Welfare Committee member Basavaraj Koravankar. The men were organizing a law enforcement strike to protest low wages and poor working conditions. The men were charged with sedition as well as various sections of Essential Services Maintenance Act (ESMA) and Police Acts. The arrested were yet to be released on bail at the time of reporting.

On September 2, more than 100 million workers across the country participated in a one-day strike in support of 12 demands that included increasing the minimum wage and a rollback of the federal government's decision to privatize the defense and railroad sectors.

b. Prohibition of Forced or Compulsory Labor

The law prohibits all forms of forced or compulsory labor, but this problem, including bonded child labor (see section 7.c.), remained widespread.

Estimates of the number of bonded laborers varied widely, although some NGOs placed the number in the tens of millions. Most bonded labor occurred in agriculture. Nonagricultural sectors with a high incidence of bonded labor were stone quarries, brick kilns, rice mills, construction, embroidery factories, and beedi (hand-rolled cigarettes) production.

Enforcement and compensation for victims is the responsibility of state and local governments and varied in effectiveness. The government generally did not effectively enforce laws related to bonded labor or labor trafficking laws, such as the Bonded Labor System (Abolition) Act. When inspectors referred violations for prosecution, court backlogs, inadequate prosecution, and a lack of prioritization sometimes resulted in acquittals. Prosecutions were rare. According to the National Crime Records Bureau, police registered 92 cases nationwide under this law in 2015.

The Ministry of Labor and Employment continued to work with the International Labor Organization to combat bonded labor, including through the "convergence program" in the states of Andhra Pradesh and Odisha to target workers vulnerable to bonded labor.

The Ministry of Labor and Employment reported the federally funded, state-run Centrally Sponsored Scheme allowed the release of 2,216 bonded laborers during the period April 2015 through March 2016. Some NGOs reported delays in obtaining release certificates for rescued bonded laborers that were required to certify employers held them in bondage and entitles them to compensation under the law. The distribution of rehabilitation funds was uneven across states. In May, the government revised its bonded labor rehabilitation program and increased the compensation for victims from 19,000 rupees ($285) to 98,000 rupees ($1,470) for male victims, 196,000 rupees ($2,940) for women and child victims, and 294,000 rupees ($4,410) for sexually exploited women and child victims.

Bonded labor, particularly in brick kilns, continued to be a concern in several states. On March 2, Tamil Nadu authorities, with assistance from an NGO, rescued more than 550 bonded laborers from a brick kiln in Tiruvallur. On May

28, authorities worked with an NGO to rescue 328 persons, including 88 children, from another Tiruvallur brick kiln.

In May an NGO, working in partnership with law enforcement officials and the People's Vigilance Committee on Human Rights, rescued 207 bonded laborers from brick kilns in Uttar Pradesh.

SC and ST members lived and worked under traditional arrangements of servitude in many areas of the country. Although the central government abolished Sulung servitude in 1964, the social group remained impoverished and vulnerable to forced exploitation in Arunachal Pradesh.

Also see the Department of State's *Trafficking in Persons Report* at www.state.gov/j/tip/rls/tiprpt/.

c. Prohibition of Child Labor and Minimum Age for Employment

The government amended the Child Labor (Abolition) Act in August to ban employment of children below the age of 14. The amended law permits employment of children between the ages of 14 and 18, except in mines. Children are prohibited from using flammable substances, explosives, or other hazardous material, as defined by the Indian Factories Act. The law, however, permits employment of children in family-owned enterprises after school hours.

State governments enforced labor laws and employed labor inspectors, while the Ministry of Labor and Employment provided oversight and coordination. Nevertheless, violations were common. The amended law establishes a penalty in the range of 20,000 rupees ($300) to 50,000 rupees ($750) per child employed in hazardous industries. Such fines were often insufficient to deter violations, and authorities sporadically enforced them. The fines are deposited in a welfare fund for formerly employed children.

The Ministry of Labor and Employment coordinated its efforts with states to raise awareness about child labor by funding various outreach events such as plays and community activities. In June children's rights NGO Bachpan Bachao Andolan and local government officials rescued 52 children from roadside eateries, grocery shops, and vehicle repairs shops in Ranchi, Jharkand.

On May 19, the Delhi government, in collaboration with the Justice Ventures International, rescued eight children from a bindi (a traditional forehead decoration) manufacturing establishment in Khajuri Khas, a North Delhi neighborhood.

Child labor remained widespread. UNICEF estimated there were 29 million child laborers between the ages of five and 18. Some NGOs estimated the number to be significantly higher. According to the national census of 2011, there were 4.5 million child laborers between the ages of five and 14. The majority of child labor occurred in agriculture and the informal economy, in particular in stone quarries, in the rolling of cigarettes, and in informal food service establishments. Commercial sexual exploitation of children occurred (see section 6, Children).

Forced child labor, including bonded labor, also remained a serious problem. Employers engaged children in forced or indentured labor as domestic servants and beggars, as well as in quarrying, brick kilns, rice mills, silk-thread production, and textile embroidery.

Also see the Department of Labor's *Findings on the Worst Forms of Child Labor* at www.dol.gov/ilab/reports/child-labor/findings/.

d. Discrimination with Respect to Employment and Occupation

The law and regulations prohibit discrimination with respect to employment and occupation, with respect to race, sex, gender, disability, language, sexual orientation, and/or gender identity, or social status. The law does not prohibit discrimination against individuals with HIV/AIDS or other communicable diseases, color, religion, political opinion, national origin or citizenship. The government effectively enforced those laws and regulations within the formal sector. The law and regulations, however, do not protect those working within the informal sector, who comprised an estimated 90 percent of the workforce.

Discrimination occurred in the informal sector with respect to Dalits, indigenous people, and persons with disabilities. Legal protections are the same for all, but gender discrimination with respect to wages was prevalent. Foreign migrant workers were largely undocumented and typically did not enjoy the protection of labor laws available to workers who are Indian nationals.

e. Acceptable Conditions of Work

Federal law sets safety and health standards, but state government laws set minimum wages, hours of work, and safety and health standards. The daily minimum wage (with local cost of living allowance included) varied from 197 rupees ($2.89) in Bihar to 447 rupees ($6.57) in Delhi. The officially estimated poverty income level was less than 27 rupees ($0.43) per day. State governments set a separate minimum wage for agricultural workers.

Laws on wages, hours, and occupational health and safety do not apply to the large informal sector.

The law mandates a maximum eight-hour workday and 48-hour workweek, as well as safe working conditions, which include provisions for restrooms, cafeterias, medical facilities, and ventilation. The law mandates a minimum rest period of 30 minutes after every four hours of work and premium pay for overtime, but it does not mandate paid holidays. The law prohibits compulsory overtime, but it does not limit the amount of overtime a worker can work. Occupational safety and health standards set by the government were generally up to date and covered the main industries in the country.

State governments are responsible for enforcing minimum wages, hours of work, and safety and health standards. The number of inspectors generally was insufficient to enforce labor law. State governments often did not effectively enforce the minimum wage law for agricultural workers. Enforcement of safety and health standards was poor, especially in the informal sector but also in some formal sector industries. Penalties for violation of occupational safety and health standards range from a fine of 100,000 rupees ($1,600) to imprisonment of up to two years, but they were not sufficient to deter violations.

Violations of wage, overtime, and occupational safety and health standards were common in the informal sector (industries and/or establishments that do not fall under the purview of the Factories Act), which employed an estimated 90 percent of the workforce. Small, low-technology factories frequently exposed workers to hazardous working conditions. Undocumented foreign workers did not receive basic occupational health and safety protections. In many instances workers could not remove themselves from situations that endangered health or safety without jeopardizing their employment.

On August 13, three untrained and unskilled sanitation workers who entered a 25-foot manhole in Hyderabad died from exposure to poisonous gases. They were reportedly not provided with proper protective gear. A passerby who tried to rescue the workers also reportedly died of asphyxiation.

According to the Asian Human Rights Commission, although the Supreme Court ordered enforcement of the 2013 Prohibition of Employment as Manual Scavengers and their Rehabilitation Act and banned the manual cleaning of sewage lines, authorities rarely implemented the act and manual scavenging persisted. The commission quoted a Dalit rights activist who asserted that at least 700 deaths in manholes occurred every year.

From January through July, eight laborers reportedly suffocated while cleaning septic tanks and manholes in Tamil Nadu.

Industrial accidents occurred frequently. On May 26, an explosion at a chemical factory killed three workers in Dombivili, near Mumbai. On July 5, an explosion in an aluminum-molding factory killed five workers in Howrah, West Bengal.